ALSO BY LORI RICE
FOOD ON TAP: COOKING WITH CRAFT BEER

Beer Bread

Brew-Infused

BREADS, ROLLS, BISCUITS, MUFFINS, AND MORE

LORI RICE

THE COUNTRYMAN PRESS

A division of W. W. Norton & Company

Independent Publishers Since 1923

For information about special discounts for bulk purchases, please contact
W. W. Norton Special Sales at specialsales@wwnorton.com or 800-233-4830

Manufacturing through Imago
Book design by Anna Reich
Production manager: Devon Zahn

The Countryman Press
www.countrymanpress.com

A division of W. W. Norton & Company, Inc.
500 Fifth Avenue, New York, NY 10110
www.wwnorton.com

978-1-68268-448-1 (pbk.)

10 9 8 7 6 5 4 3 2 1

To Dixie and Macy.

Thank you for showing me that there
is nothing better than a canine
coworker and that all breweries are
best visited with a dog.

CONTENTS

INTRODUCTION

If one were trying to come up with a list of the most desirable foods and drinks that require the fewest number of ingredients, beer and bread would be at the top of it. In its most basic form, bread can be made with grain, water, and yeast, and beer is created with grain, water, yeast, and hops. The two have much in common and it is why beer can be a versatile ingredient in bread-making for flavors and textures that spark adventure and curiosity.

Beer bread is not an uncommon phenomenon. For years, variations have existed. They range from three-ingredient recipes using only beer, butter, and self-rising flour to the more complex creations I've been introduced to during my travels, like the dark, grainy breads made with Guinness and served alongside comforting soups in Dublin.

With these experiences and recipes at its core, *Beer Bread* takes a classic concept and puts a twist on the ordinary and the traditional. There are many ways to reinvent breads with ingredients, styles, shapes, and serving suggestions. Similarly, the number of craft beers available to consumers today feels endless. Baking with beer allows the opportunity to support your local brewery while experimenting in the kitchen.

If you are new to baking, this book has plenty of simple, straightforward recipes, including a few creative takes on the classic beer bread with fewer than five ingredients. Along with that are some more elaborate breads and baking techniques, like braided loaves for more advanced bakers. If you are new to beer, that will not be a challenge either. For many recipes, multiple types of beers can be used, so you can grab what you are familiar with or branch out and try something new.

This book aims to be a good fit for anyone interested in bread and beer by exploring baking to create new flavors in innovative ways. The result is tempting, modern recipes for approachable, freshly baked breads at home.

I hope your taste buds are ready because they are about to go on an unforgettable adventure.

Chapter I

BAKING BREAD IOI

The difficulty, ingredients needed, and time required to bake bread varies by the type of loaf you want to pull out of the oven. It's true that baking requires a more precise measurement of ingredients and more specific tools than cooking, but this shouldn't scare you if you feel inexperienced. Preparing breads for baking is really a simple and—for many—therapeutic and rewarding process. Once you grow familiar with the basic steps, it only gets easier from there.

The goal of this book isn't to teach you how to bake, but to show you creative ways to do so with beer. With that in mind, it is still helpful to do a brief overview of the *what* and *why* of bread baking so that I can share some tips I've found useful over the years and provide some explanations regarding methods and recipes in this book.

TYPES OF BREADS IN THIS BOOK

The breads and variations of breads—such as flatbreads, biscuits, and rolls—can be classified into two categories: yeast breads and quick breads. Yeast breads tend to be the scariest for beginner bakers and sometimes the most finicky for even the experienced, so let's start by discussing why this is often the case. Then we'll move on to quick breads. Both produce equally enjoyable results, but hopefully some basic tips and guidelines will help you decide where you want to start as you dig into these beer bread recipes.

YEAST BREADS

Yeast breads require the three main ingredients of flour, yeast, and a liquid. In basic versions that liquid is water, but as you may have guessed, the liquid in our case will be beer. There are several steps in making yeast breads and each plays an important role in achieving the desired recipe results.

Mixing: When the ingredients are mixed, enzymes begin to break down starch molecules into sugars that will feed the yeast. Mixing the ingredients is the initial step in facilitating the fermentation process, when yeast produces the carbon dioxide and alcohol that contribute to the structure and flavor of your bread.

Kneading: Kneading dough, whether done by hand or with a mixer, helps to develop the proteins in the dough, called the gluten network. This network traps the air bubbles given off by the yeast to give bread strength and a desirable rise and texture.

I find hand-kneading meditative, but I also understand that it can be time consuming and sometimes frustrating when you are working with a stickier dough. For most yeast breads in this book, you will find the general instructions to knead the dough in an electric stand mixer for 5 minutes and then knead by hand for 3 to 4 additional minutes. Doughs that have fat added like butter or oil and sweeteners like sugar often require longer kneading times and they can sometimes be very sticky until the kneading is complete. In these cases, I often suggest doing it all in the mixer. It really doesn't matter how you work the dough, just that the gluten is fully developed after kneading.

Rising: The rising stage for bread is also called proofing, and that is how I refer to it in this book. Once you knead a dough, it's formed into a ball and placed in a greased bowl. It can then be covered with a cloth bowl cover, dish towel, loose lid, or even a shower cap to rest. During this proofing stage is when fermentation occurs. The yeast does its thing, producing carbon dioxide and alcohol that will create the crumb and structure of the bread. It also contributes to the aroma and flavor.

Proofing a loaf of bread is both a straightforward and a tricky step. A bread dough with healthy yeast is going to rise, but how quickly and how much is where bakers sometimes run into problems. The reason is that room temperature affects how quickly dough rises.

The ideal temperature for proofing the doughs in this book during fermentation is around 75 to 80°F, but the temperature of your room can vary. Perhaps it's a chilly winter morning or maybe the oven has been running all day and your kitchen is warmer. I often put dough in my pantry in the winter because it provides a warm, draft-free spot, but in the summer it runs a few degrees warmer than my already-warm kitchen so it's not a good option.

These temperature differences aren't a problem; they just mean that you have to do a bit of personal troubleshooting when baking yeast breads. Breads will take longer to rise or may rise faster than instructions in a recipe state. Many recipes also state that dough should double in size. All of these indicators should be taken as estimates. In reality some loaves only rise about 50 percent. It's just that "until doubled in size" and "about 1 hour" have become common language in recipe writing and baking instruction.

I include these instructions in each recipe but remember that they may vary depending on the temperature of your space. Over time you will become familiar with your baking environment and what that means for a successful loaf.

Baking: It can be difficult to tell when yeast breads are fully baked because the outer crust can look done when the interior still has a bit of time to go. Unlike quick breads, which I discuss later, you can't stick a toothpick all the way in to check that the dough is baked. A kitchen thermometer is essential. Exact temperatures are listed in each recipe, but in general I bake yeast breads with eggs, sugar, and butter to 190°F and others to 175 to 180°F. The temperature of yeast breads will often continue to climb once they're pulled from the oven so it's okay to remove them when they are within about 3 degrees of the goal.

QUICK BREADS

These breads are given their names because they do not use yeast and do not require the time necessary for kneading and proofing. Their leavening agents are typically baking soda and baking powder. Making them isn't much different than baking a cake. You simply stir together the ingredients, pour it in a prepared loaf pan, and bake. Because they are batter based, they do often take longer to bake, which can make the name *quick bread* feel a little deceiving. While some yeast breads take as little as 20 minutes to bake, some quick breads can take up to 60 minutes.

BAKING TOOLS

Before getting started, it is helpful to make sure you have all the tools you need to make the recipes in this book. You obviously don't need them all to make every recipe, but many are essential to the process.

Electric Mixer (Stand Mixer) with a Dough Hook: This makes mixing ingredients and kneading dough easy. I consider it essential to bread baking in my kitchen.

Ingredient Scale: Weighing flour is essential to the success of these recipes and I encourage it over using cup measurements. I explain more about this in the next section when we discuss flour. You will also need a scale to weigh pieces of dough for rolls, to ensure they are the same size.

Volume Measuring Cup: Beer will be measured in ounces and a standard cup you'd use to measure out dry ingredients like sugar is different than those used for measuring volume in liquid ounces.

Large Glass Bowl: What your bread proofs in can affect the temperature and the speed of fermentation and rising. For example, metal can stay cool, which means it's not a good idea to leave a dough in the bowl of many electric mixers to rise. You can use special proofing baskets, but I prefer glass bowls greased with butter or cooking oil.

Kitchen Brush: Many breads get a brush of egg wash before being baked. I often use rubber kitchen brushes because many can be washed in the dishwasher to sanitize.

Dough Scraper: Plastic will do, but I prefer metal to help cut pieces of dough. They are also helpful for scraping up flour and bits of dough off the countertop after kneading for easier cleanup.

Parchment Paper: I use parchment on all my baking sheets to keep breads from sticking and to make cleanup easier. If you are baking a lot, the pre-cut sheets will save you loads of time and they tend to lay flatter in the pan than pieces from a roll.

Sheet Pans: I bake rolls and many yeast breads on a standard rimmed baking sheet. Quarter sheet pans are great for smaller recipes with only six rolls.

Five- or Six-Quart Dutch Oven: You'll need this for the no-knead bread recipes.

Loaf Pans: Two sizes are used throughout this book: 8½-by-4½ inches and 9-by-5 inches.

Baking Dishes: A few recipes call for baking dishes and a standard 9-by-13 inch will work fine.

Pizza Stone: I bake several yeast breads and pizzas or flatbreads on a pizza stone. If you don't have one, you can heat up a sheet pan or pizza pan as instructed, but the stone produces more authentic, crusty results.

Cooking Oil, Butter, Olive Oil, or Nonstick Spray: While also ingredients, these items become tools for baking when they assist with getting doughs and breads out of their bowls and pans. For the most part, they can be used interchangeably, although I'd stick with the first three versus spray for bowls used in proofing. Also, keep in mind flavor when deciding which to use. For example, olive oil isn't the best choice when baking sweet doughs. When used for greasing purposes I don't list them in the ingredient lists but know you will need some form or the other for most recipes.

Spray Bottle: One way to get the blistered, crispy crust of an artisanal loaf in a home oven is to bake the loaf on a pizza stone and to spritz the oven with water just before shutting the oven door to create some steam.

Aluminum Foil: Many breads brown quickly during baking. To prevent the exterior of a loaf from becoming too dark, or even burnt, before it has finished baking all the way through, you will find instructions to tent the loaf with a piece of aluminum foil. Simply tear off a sheet a little longer than the loaf. Create a crease in the middle so it is like a tent and gently place it over the loaf 20 to 30 minutes into its baking time.

Oven Thermometer: Knowing the true temperature of your oven will help with accurate baking times. If you find your oven runs warmer or cooler than what the setting is indicating, you can adjust for it by changing your setting accordingly. For example, if you preheat your oven to 350°F and find that it is only heating to 325°F, you can set it to 375°F to accommodate the discrepancy.

Kitchen Thermometer: As mentioned before, this tool will allow you to determine when yeast breads are ready to come out of the oven.

IMPORTANT NOTES ON INGREDIENTS, AMOUNTS, AND MEASURING

THE TYPE AND AMOUNT OF YEAST

I use active dry yeast for all recipes that require the leavening agent. While any type of baking yeast will work, you will need to substitute the amount correctly based on the type of yeast you use. The yeast's label or the company's website often have a conversion chart that is easily accessible.

I use active dry yeast for two reasons. First, it's easy to obtain at the supermarket. Second, it also doesn't require a step to bloom the yeast. I will admit that one of my favorite steps of traditional bread baking is allowing the yeast to bloom (bubble and foam) in warm water with sugar, but I wanted these recipes to be as simple as possible. Active dry yeast is equally effective when added to the dry ingredients and mixed into the dough, so that is how it is used in this book.

If you fear that your yeast may be old and no longer effective, I would encourage you to test it before adding it to the other ingredients. For the test, add some warm water (105 to 110°F) to a bowl with a tablespoon of sugar. Add a teaspoon of the yeast. If it blooms with bubbles and foam on top within 5 minutes, it is active and can be used in the recipe.

If you don't bake all the time you likely don't keep large quantities of yeast in the house. Most occasional bakers buy yeast in the small ¼-ounce packets sold at the supermarket. While I often purchase yeast by the jar now, I used to buy those packets, too. I always hated having a half-full packet left over because, no matter how well I tried to seal it, it would inevitably get knocked around in the pantry and spill yeast on the shelves. To eliminate this problem and further simplify beer bread baking, I made sure each recipe in this book uses 2¼ teaspoons of yeast, which is the amount in one ¼-ounce packet.

TYPES OF FLOUR AND MEASUREMENTS

It took me a long time to come around to weighing dry ingredients. I preferred to bake like my grandmothers and mother, and I don't ever remember a scale being around. I changed my habits a bit when writing this book. I find weighing the flour essential to consistent results. It ensures that the doughs come together as expected, such as on the dryer side or slightly sticky, which varies according to the type of bread being prepared.

You will find a variety of flours used in this book, including all-purpose, bread flour, self-rising flour, white whole wheat, Irish wholemeal, and rye. While there are many sources out there that sell these flours, I use King Arthur Flour products, so the measurements are based on their weight chart for flour types. For example, all-purpose flour is 120 grams per cup. Following the weight measurements for the recipes will allow you to use any brand of flours that you prefer.

EGG WASH

Most breads need a brush of some type of liquid that will result in a golden-brown crust when baked. Egg wash is my preference. To avoid listing the water and egg in every ingredient list, I simply have "egg wash" when it is needed. Many recipes call for one tablespoon of water to one large egg. I like to use 2 teaspoons of water to one large egg, but either will do. You likely won't use it all if you are only baking one loaf. I find it stores a day or two in the fridge if I plan to bake more soon.

Chapter 2

BAKING BREAD WITH BEER

In this book, beer replaces common liquids used in bread baking, such as water. In addition to hydrating the dough, beer has two major roles in baking. Beer assists with leavening. While it's true that beer contains yeast, by the time a bottle reaches your hands that yeast is no longer active, making carbonation the main player in beer's influence on the texture of your bread. Beer also enhances richness and flavor. There are a few general rules when baking with beer that involve the type of beer being used, how it is added, and enjoying the breads when they are at their peak freshness.

AMOUNT OF BEER

I wanted each recipe in this book to be approachable and straightforward. I thought the best way to achieve that was to streamline the ingredients throughout each chapter. I already mentioned the consistency with the yeast and I did the same for the beer.

After my first book, *Food on Tap: Cooking with Craft Beer*, I looked back and saw how many recipes used 2 ounces of beer here and 9 ounces there. While necessary for each recipe, they were odd amounts that left random volumes of beer unused.

It had me wondering if readers found this frustrating. So, I did a small survey through social media. My question was, "Would you rather have a larger amount of bread from a recipe that uses a full 12-ounce beer, or would you prefer a smaller yield and to use only 6 ounces, or half of a beer?"

The results were a solid fifty-fifty. Some prefer having half of a beer to drink while others like to use every bit of it in the recipe. So I used both amounts, but only two volumes without small splashes here or nearly full beers there. Each of the recipes in this book uses either 6 ounces of beer or 12 ounces of beer, so you will know what to expect. You'll also know that, if you only have one bottle of a beer around, you have enough to get baking.

ADDING BEER TO A RECIPE

Room temperature beer is necessary for all the recipes in this book. In yeast breads this helps to encourage the yeast activity while a chilled beer would retard its activity. In quick breads, this will prevent other ingredients like melted butter from solidifying due to contact with a chilled liquid.

It's best to pour the beer and to let the foam settle before adding it to the other ingredients. This is especially important when using only 6 ounces, to ensure accurate measurement. I will admit that I have made plenty of the recipes that use 12 ounces of beer by pouring it straight from the bottle or can and things worked out just fine. You might have to wait a bit for the foam to settle in the mixer, but otherwise there should be no negative effects if you happen to be in a rush.

Beer is an acidic ingredient so the way it is added to quick breads requires a little care. If dumped in all at once in the early stages of the recipe it can cause curdling of other delicate ingredients. To combat this, the beer is added at the end and alternated with adding dry ingredients about one-third of each at a time. I find this results in a silky-smooth batter for baking.

With yeast breads, this is less of a concern, but you will find that the beer is added to the yeast and flour for ease of mixing and dough formation before other flavorings like salt and sugar go in.

STORAGE AND SHELF-LIFE OF BEER BREADS

Beer enhances the flavors and textures of breads and baked goods, but it can behave in different ways as the freshness fades. This is highly dependent on the type of bread. As the flavors of beer settle, the maltiness can strengthen and overpower other ingredients. In an effort not to repeat the same guidelines recipe after recipe, follow the general rule—eat all the items in this book the day they are baked for optimum flavor and texture. Store any that you choose to save as you would any bread or baked goods: in an airtight bag or container, unless instructions state otherwise.

Yeast breads are best when warm or at room temperature and eaten fresh, but they will hang on in flavor longer than quick breads, often two to three days. During this time, they may become dryer. Consider enjoying them as sides and snacks on the first day and then they make delicious toast and French toast the following days.

Quick breads are best eaten at room temperature or only slightly warm. The flavors tend to have a better balance as the bread cools. Whether sweet or savory, they are more like cakes, and it's best to adhere to the rule of eating them the day they are baked for best results. If you'd like them to hang on with freshness a bit longer, slice and freeze for use over a few days and thaw a few hours before you plan to eat it. Freezing helps preserve the flavor balance before the settling beer flavors take over.

BEERS FOR BAKING BREAD

The intricate flavors of beer tend to be less pronounced in baked bread than when cooking with beer. You will find that the strength of the beer's flavors control whether hints of fruit, chocolate, or coffee are pulled into the final loaf. But for the most part beer is there for a deep richness and slight malty or boozy flavor, as well as for its cooperation with the yeast for leavening.

In general, beers that have a less pronounced hop profile are best for baking. That's because hops tend to turn bitter at high baking temperatures and during long baking times. (But don't swear off hoppy beers just yet. I'll explain below.) Some beers that create great baking results include blonde ales, brown ales, märzens (oktoberfest), amber ales, porters, and stouts. These beers tend to have IBU levels that are 40 and lower. IBU stands for International Bitterness Unit and it is a general measurement for perceived bitterness of a beer. It provides a clue to the balance of hops to other ingredients and a higher number most often means you have a hoppy beer on your hands, which translates to bitterness during baking.

If you read *Food on Tap*, though, you know I'm a fan of experimentation, and that I don't always view pleasant bitterness as a bad thing. Neither do many craft beer fans out there, or the West Coast IPA (India Pale Ale) would not be such a popular style. Given that, I feel there is a place for a hoppier beer in baking. So you will find IPAs and pale ales in a few breads in this book. I wouldn't reach for a beer that is nearly off the charts at something like 90 IBUs, but I tend to enjoy a cheesy beer bread that uses a beer that falls within 40 to 70 IBUs.

For example, the Cheese and Herb Pale Ale Bread (page 153) is a twist on the classic beer bread that uses self-rising flour. Traditional versions use a plain lager or American light lager, which results in a hint of beer flavor, but not much of a punch. In this variation, I love to use a hoppy pale ale because the slight bitterness goes so well with the Cheddar that melts beautifully over the loaf as it bakes.

Styles of beer you won't find in this book are the super boozy barrel-aged beer or those that are often titled imperial, such as imperial IPA or imperial stout. The strong flavors of these beers and their high alcohol content tend to overpower other flavors, disrupting the intended balance. There are some exceptions along the way, but the beers I find that are the best for baking are usually less than 7 percent alcohol.

Due to the hint of flavor that beer adds to breads, the baker has a lot of flexibility. In this book you will find recipes that specify the beer style as well as others that simply call for beer with a variety of suggestions included. So instead of making a list of each style of beer used, I decided it would be more helpful to group them. In terms of tasting notes, these groups do generalize the beer styles, and a few might fit into a couple of different categories, but when it comes to making beer bread these groups categorize flavor characteristics. So when you are making a bread and you don't have a beer that a recipe specifically suggests, you can refer to this chapter and easily find a substitute.

I should also mention that I like baking with more classic styles of beer, which means I've worked a lot of German and Belgian styles into this book. They tend to have more of the mellow savory flavors and moderate sweetness that work well in breads, versus the trends in bold innovation—meant to pleasantly shock the taste buds—that tend to take over the market in the United States. Those hazy IPAs and shocking sours are delicious for drinking, and I do manage to infuse them into a recipe or two, but dunkels, dubbels, golden ales, pilsners, bitters, and brown ales are much more versatile in baking. That being said, some local craft breweries are making excellent re-creations of these more historic styles of beer. That makes it well worth taking a look around and grabbing a growler when you can. If you struggle to find these styles in your area don't be afraid to hop over to the international section of the beer store. I promise not to tell. I do it all the time.

LIGHTLY FLAVORED AND VERSATILE

Styles: Blonde ale, lager, pale lager, American light lager, Asian-style lager, Indian-style lager, Mexican lager

These beers are light in color and body and offer less bold flavors. They pair well with vibrantly flavored foods because they serve a supporting role and don't compete with the food. Similarly, in bread recipes they let you know that beer is there, but they don't take over other ingredients. If you aren't a fan of bold beer flavors, you might want to start with this category. With the exception of recipes that call for porters and stouts, these styles can be used in any recipe in the book.

NUTTY OR SLIGHTLY SWEET AND MALTY WITH TOFFEE, CARAMEL, OR TOASTED NOTES

Styles: Amber ale (red ale), brown ale, bière de garde, black ale, black lager, cream ale, dark ale, doppelbock, dunkel, English bitter, märzen (oktoberfest), Vienna lager

Beers with these characteristics are used in recipes that have a touch of sweetness from brown sugar or dried fruits. But their toasted notes also support more savory creations with ingredients like sausage and mushrooms. A couple of outliers in the group are the English Bitter, which can be hoppier than the others, and the cream ale that, without the addition of something like vanilla, can be very light in flavor. I find that they work well as substitutes in the recipes using other beers in this list, so I've kept them in this category.

CRISP AND REFRESHING WITH MALTY NOTES

Styles: Helles, kölsch, pilsner

These bright and refreshing beers are of German and Czech origin and you will find many used accordingly in the book. They work well for recipes that need a light hint of flavor with the maltiness that lets you know beer has been included.

SLIGHTLY SWEET AND BOOZY

Styles: Belgian blonde ale, Belgian dubbel, Belgian golden ale, Belgian strong ale, Scotch ale

Belgian beers have a boozy sweetness that is unique to the region and they add a boost of flavor to baked goods and breads. I keep Scotch ale in this category due to its characteristic booziness and bold flavor. Be sure to keep an eye on the alcohol content of these beers when making a selection as many will hover around 7 percent and higher. Stick to the lower end.

DARK WITH ROASTED CHOCOLATE AND COFFEE NOTES

Styles: Porter, chocolate porter, coconut porter, stout, chocolate stout, coffee stout, Irish stout, milk stout, oatmeal stout

These beers are richly flavored, but despite their color, they can range from light bodied to heavy. They are used in both sweet and savory recipes throughout the book. When making substitutions be sure to use a standard variety, such as a stout or Irish stout, for savory recipes, and don't mistakenly pick up a chocolate stout, which will have a sweetness that could clash with other ingredients.

WARMING AND SPICED

Styles: Holiday ale, pumpkin ale, spiced ale, winter lager, winter warmer

Any type of beer that is spiced with ingredients common during the holidays falls into this category. It also includes seasonal twists like beers made with pumpkin or sweet potatoes. These beers are most often used in sweeter breads. Unless the beer is heavily spiced, little of it will come through in the bread on its own, but if you don't like the spices of the season, try swapping a brown ale or amber ale for any recipe that calls for a spiced holiday beer.

FRUITY AND SEASONAL

Styles: Fruit ale, fruit wheat, beers made with wine or grape must, strawberry blonde, gose

These beers can show up year-round, but most often fruit beers align with summer months, when the berries used to make them are also in season. Fruit beers can range from the super sweet to a beer that offers the essence of the fruit without syrupy sweetness. I include beers made in wine barrels or with grapes in this category because they often take on the sweetness of the fruit. An outlier here is the gose, which will be the tartest of the group and slightly salty, but most are enhanced with fruit flavors so it fits well in this category for baking.

HOPPY AND PLEASANTLY BITTER WITH FLORAL OR CITRUS NOTES

Styles: IPA, pale ale

If a recipe calls for an IPA or pale ale, stick with that category if you want a bit of the balanced bitterness that comes from the hops. The creativity comes in with beers that have been flavored with fruits. For example, some recipes call for tropical IPAs. These are often brewed with mango, passion fruit, citrus, guava, and pineapple. Many are strongly flavored and I do find that they come through in the taste of many quick breads.

CRISP AND HERBAL WITH CITRUS OR OTHER FRUIT NOTES

Styles: American wheat, hazy or Northeast IPAs, hefeweizen, saison, white ale, witbier

This category is for the refreshing wheat and white ales that are often unfiltered, making them golden and slightly hazy in appearance. They drop hints of citrus, sometimes more tropical banana, and herbs like coriander with each sip. I also include the Hazy IPA, also called a Northeastern IPA, New England IPA, or NE IPA, in this category. This is because, despite the fact that they are IPAs, they are often low in bitterness and extremely juicy to a point where they resemble orange juice in both appearance and taste. These qualities allow them to work well for substitutions among this group.

Chapter 3

START THE DAY
BREAKFAST BREADS, BISCUITS, AND MUFFINS

Whether it's an average morning or a special occasion, these breads and baked goods will start the day off right. Craft beer is used in batters and doughs to give a creative twist to breakfast classics while also introducing some new ideas. The recipes progress from sweet to savory, so there is something for every appetite.

Classic Beer Bread Vanilla Scones with Honey Glaze

I've had many types of scones and I can't remember disliking any of them! I was first introduced to the breakfast pastry during my days working in a bakery. There we made a soft, imperfectly shaped style that was a bit more like a biscuit than the dryer (but equally delicious) version I was later introduced to in Europe. These scones put a twist on the Classic Beer Bread recipe (page 150) to mimic those first scones I encountered. The best part is that they are easy to stir up and bake, even on a busy morning. Choose a light, less hoppy beer for these scones. I like using a witbier or a simple lager.

MAKES 10 SCONES

452 grams (4 cups) self-rising flour
½ cup currants, dried cranberries, or raisins
½ cup sugar
1 teaspoon lemon zest
¼ teaspoon ground vanilla bean
3 tablespoons unsalted butter, melted
12 ounces (1½ cups) beer

GLAZE
½ cup powdered sugar, sifted
1 tablespoon honey
4 teaspoons half-and-half or milk
Pinch of fine sea salt

Stir together the flour, currants, sugar, lemon zest, and vanilla bean in a large bowl. Stir in the butter. Pour in the beer and stir until a thick batter forms. Preheat the oven to 400°F. Let the dough rest for 15 minutes while the oven heats.

Line a large baking sheet with parchment paper. Scoop out the batter by about ⅓-cup portions and spoon onto the baking sheet, with a maximum of six scones at a time. Bake 20 minutes, until the edges are golden brown. Repeat with the remaining batter. Transfer the baked scones to a cooling rack to cool completely.

Stir together all of the glaze ingredients and drizzle over the scones. Let the glaze set about 10 minutes before serving.

Find a Beer: Allagash Brewing Company White, Avery Brewing Company White Rascal, Firestone Walker Brewing Company Lager

Date and Dunkel Morning Buns

A sweet bread made with a dark and malty German Dunkel is paired with rich dates and cinnamon in these breakfast buns. I have the luxury of access to local dates at my farmers' market, as 90 percent of the country's dates are grown in California. If you are not as lucky, choose whole pitted dates and chop them yourself, instead of pre-chopped dates from the supermarket, which have a coating to prevent clumping. You also might need to pulse the dates in a food processor to create a paste.

MAKES 8 BUNS

360 grams (3 cups) all-purpose flour

2¼ teaspoons (one ¼-ounce packet) active dry yeast

¼ cup sugar

6 ounces (¾ cup) German dunkel

4 tablespoons (½ stick) unsalted butter, melted

1 large egg

½ teaspoon fine sea salt

1 cup pitted dates, finely chopped

¼ cup light brown sugar

½ teaspoon ground cinnamon

Egg wash

½ tablespoon coarse ground sugar or sanding sugar

Add the flour, yeast, and sugar to the bowl of a stand mixer fitted with the dough hook. Turn the mixer to low and pour in the beer. Scrape the sides of the bowl as needed and mix until a dough begins to form. Mix in the butter, and then add the egg. Mix in the salt.

Allow the mixer to knead the dough for 10 minutes. The dough will be slightly sticky but should not stick to your fingers. Transfer it to a flat surface and form into a ball. Place the ball of dough in a bowl that has been greased with butter. Cover it and let it proof until it's doubled in size, 60 to 90 minutes.

While the dough proofs, add the dates to a medium bowl. Add the brown sugar and cinnamon. Use a fork to mash all the ingredients into a paste. If your dates are too firm, transfer them to a single-serve blender or small food processer to blend into a paste.

Punch down the dough and turn it out onto a floured surface. Use a rolling pin to roll it to a rectangle about 13-by-18 inches.

Gently spread the date paste over the left half of the rectangle, leaving about a ½ inch on all sides. It may be clumpy in spots and that is fine. Spread it as evenly as you can.

Next fold the right half over the date paste. Gently roll the new rectangle to about 9-by-16 inches. Working on the long side, cut the layered dough into eight strips, each 2 inches wide.

For each strip, twist it and then fold it into a knot, tucking the ends under. Place the buns on a baking sheet covered in parchment paper. Preheat the oven to 350°F and allow the rolls to proof on top of the oven for 30 minutes.

Brush the rolls with egg wash and sprinkle with coarse sugar. Bake for 25 minutes, until golden brown. Serve warm or at room temperature.

Find a Beer: Kansas City Bier Company Dunkel, Surly Brewing Company Schadenfreude, Victory Brewing Company Dark Lager

Chicken and Waffle Donut Bites with Märzen Maple Syrup

Chicken and waffles is one of those meals that is constantly being reinvented. All the creative interpretations I encounter got me thinking: How could I pair chicken and waffles with beer and make it a treat that would also fall into the bread category? The answer is these donut bites! Leftover shredded chicken is stirred into a waffle batter made with beer and dropped into the deep fryer to create golden breakfast bites. It's something that reminds me of the fair food served at the renowned Fall Festival near my hometown in Evansville, Indiana. The festival occurs every October, so, in choosing the beer for the batter, an oktoberfest or märzen seem like a good fit for both their seasonality and roasted, caramelized flavors.

SERVES 6 TO 8

240 grams (2 cups) all-purpose flour

¼ cup sugar

2 teaspoons baking powder

½ teaspoon fine sea salt

12 ounces (1½ cups) märzen

1 tablespoon unsalted butter, melted

1 large egg

2 cups shredded, seasoned chicken (such as leftover rotisserie chicken)

32 ounces (4 cups) peanut oil for frying

½ cup pure maple syrup

Powdered sugar

Stir together the flour, sugar, baking powder, and salt in a medium mixing bowl. Pour in 10 ounces (1¼ cups) of the beer and stir to combine all ingredients. Stir in the butter and then the egg. Fold in the chicken and then let the batter rest for 30 minutes.

Add the oil to an electric fryer and heat it to 375°F. Drop the batter by ¼-cup measurements into the oil, working two to three at a time, careful not to overcrowd the fryer. Fry for 2 to 3 minutes on each side, until the donut bites are cooked through. Use a slotted spoon to transfer them to a plate or sheet pan covered in paper towels.

When you have some downtime in frying, heat the remaining 2 ounces (¼ cup) of beer over medium heat in a small saucepan. Allow it to come to a low boil and cook, stirring often, for 5 minutes. It should reduce to about ¾ ounce. Whisk the reduced beer into the maple syrup in a small dish.

Dust the donut bites with powdered sugar and serve warm with the beer syrup.

 **Find a Beer:** Flying Dog Brewery Dogtoberfest Märzen, Great Lakes Brewing Company Oktoberfest, Sierra Nevada Brewing Company Oktoberfest

Baked Mexican Chocolate Stout Donuts

These stout cake donuts are infused with chocolate, cinnamon, and chile powder. Use a chocolate and coffee stout and dark cocoa powder if you can find them. They make the donuts especially rich and complement the bold spices. I like to use a hot chile powder so that some heat comes through in the donuts, but mild works well, too.

MAKES 9 DONUTS

120 grams (1 cup) all-purpose flour
1 teaspoon baking powder
1 teaspoon chile powder
1 teaspoon ground cinnamon
½ teaspoon fine sea salt
4 tablespoons (½ stick) unsalted
    butter, melted
⅓ cup sugar
2 large eggs
½ teaspoon vanilla extract
¼ cup unsweetened cocoa powder
6 ounces (¾ cup) stout

GLAZE
1 cup powdered sugar, sifted
3 tablespoons unsweetened cocoa
    powder
¼ teaspoon ground cinnamon
¼ teaspoon chile powder
Pinch of fine sea salt
3 tablespoons milk (any variety)

Preheat the oven to 350°F.

Stir together the flour, baking powder, chile powder, cinnamon, and salt in a small bowl.

Add the melted butter and sugar to a separate bowl and stir well. Mix in the eggs and then the vanilla. Add the cocoa powder and stir until smooth. Stir in about one-third of the dry ingredients into the wet ingredients and then one-third of the beer. Continue to alternate between dry ingredients and beer until all has been added. Stir well. It's okay if it seems slightly lumpy.

Pour the batter into the nine slots of a nonstick or silicone donut pan. (Two pans will be required if using a six-donut pan.) Bake for 12 to 14 minutes, until the donuts are firm in the center. Let the donuts cool for 10 minutes, then remove them from the pan and transfer to a cooling rack to cool completely.

To make the glaze, stir together the powdered sugar, cocoa powder, cinnamon, chile powder, and salt in a shallow dish. Stir in the milk a tablespoon at a time until a smooth glaze results.

Set the cooling rack with the donuts over a sheet pan or piece of parchment paper for easier cleanup. Dip the top of each donut in the glaze. You will have plenty of glaze, so coat them generously. Set the donuts back on the cooling rack, glaze side up. Allow them to sit for at least 5 minutes to set the glaze before serving.

Find a Beer: Copper Kettle Brewing Company Mexican Chocolate Stout, Stone Brewing Xocoveza, New Realm Brewing Company Oaxaca Choca

Hazy IPA Orange Muffins

I am a huge fan of these muffins because they are simple to stir together on a busy morning. The result is bright orange flavors in a buttery, tender baked good. The hazy IPA, or Northeast IPA, is known for being a fruity beer that is low in bitterness. The style is often compared to orange juice and described as juicy or hazy. It's the perfect style of beer to use in a citrus muffin!

MAKES 8 MUFFINS

180 grams (1½ cups) all-purpose flour

1½ tablespoons orange zest (about 3 small oranges)

1 teaspoon baking powder

½ teaspoon baking soda

½ teaspoon fine sea salt

4 tablespoons (½ stick) unsalted butter, melted

½ cup sugar

1 large egg

6 ounces (¾ cup) hazy IPA

GLAZE

5 tablespoons powdered sugar, sifted

1 ounce (2 tablespoons) fresh orange juice

Pinch of fine sea salt

Preheat the oven to 400°F. Grease eight slots of a 12-muffin tin with butter or cooking oil.

Toss together the flour, orange zest, baking powder, baking soda, and salt in a small bowl.

Stir together the melted butter and the sugar in a separate medium bowl. Stir in the egg. Add about one-third of the dry ingredients and stir well, then add about one-third of the beer, continuing to alternate with dry ingredients and beer until all ingredients are stirred into a batter.

Divide the batter into the eight prepared slots of the muffin tin, filling each to about three-quarters full. Bake for 20 minutes, until the edges are browned and a toothpick inserted into the center of a muffin comes out clean. Let them cool for 10 minutes.

Make the glaze while the muffins cool. Stir the powdered sugar into the orange juice, one tablespoon at a time to create a smooth, thin glaze. Stir in the salt.

Remove the muffins from the tin and place them on a cooling rack set over a sheet pan or a piece of parchment paper. Spoon a generous teaspoon of the glaze over each of the muffins and spread it so it soaks into the top and drapes the sides. Enjoy the muffins warm or at room temperature.

 Find a Beer: Deschutes Brewery Fresh Haze IPA, New Belgium Brewing Company Voodoo Ranger Juicy Haze IPA, Sierra Nevada Brewing Company Hazy Little Thing IPA

Six-Pack Cinnamon Rolls

These cinnamon rolls are baked in half-pint, wide-mouth mason jars, creating a convenient grab-and-go breakfast or a fun way to add some character to a beer-tasting brunch.

Several beer styles will work well to create a tender, sweet dough. The basic lager is a solid choice, but don't be afraid to branch out to a brown ale or spiced beer. You'll need a little patience with these rolls in two ways. First, the dough rests and rises in the refrigerator for 20 to 24 hours. Second, it is a sticky dough, so use generously floured hands and surface to work with it. It's worth it in the end, I promise!

MAKES 6 ROLLS

330 grams (2¾ cups) all-purpose flour
2¼ teaspoons (one ¼-ounce packet) active dry yeast
6 ounces (¾ cup) lager, brown ale, or spiced beer
½ cup sugar
4 tablespoons (½ stick) unsalted butter, softened at room temperature
1 large egg
1 teaspoon fine sea salt
½ teaspoon vanilla extract

Add the flour and yeast to the bowl of a stand mixer fitted with the dough hook. Turn it to low and pour in the beer. Scrape the sides of the bowl as needed and mix until a dough begins to form. Mix in the sugar, butter, and egg. Add the salt and vanilla. Continue to mix until a very sticky dough forms.

Scrape the sides of the bowl often and allow the mixer to knead the dough for 10 minutes. It will continue to be sticky but will become smooth as the mixer kneads it.

Grease a bowl with butter or cooking oil. Transfer the dough to the prepared bowl, cover, and refrigerate for 20 to 24 hours.

Just before you remove the dough from the refrigerator, preheat the oven to 350°F. Grease six wide-mouth, half-pint mason jars with butter. Prepare a well-floured surface.

Turn the dough out of the bowl and use floured hands to form it into a ball. Roll out to a rectangle about 8-by-12 inches with the 12-inch side facing you. Continue to sprinkle the top and bottom with flour as you roll. It's important to work quickly so the dough remains chilled and easy to work with.

For the filling, brush the melted butter over the rectangle of dough. Sprinkle it with the brown sugar, cinnamon, and nuts, if using. Roll the dough toward you, tossing flour under it as you roll or using a scraper if necessary. Place it seam side down; it will be soft and loose in shape.

Find a Beer: Firestone Walker Brewing Company Lager, Brooklyn Brewery Brooklyn Brown Ale, Anchor Brewing Company Christmas Ale

continued

FILLING

2 tablespoons unsalted butter, melted

¼ cup brown sugar

1 teaspoon ground cinnamon

¼ cup chopped nuts (optional)

FROSTING

¾ cup powdered sugar, sifted

1 tablespoon unsalted butter, softened at room temperature

2 tablespoons sour cream

½ teaspoon vanilla extract

Pinch of fine sea salt

Tuck in the ends and cut it into six rolls, each about 2 inches wide. Transfer each roll, cut side up, into a prepared mason jar.

Place the mason jars on a baking sheet and bake for 30 to 35 minutes, until golden brown on the top and the interior of the rolls reaches 190°F. Allow them to cool for 10 minutes.

Make the frosting by using a fork to mash together the powdered sugar with the butter in a small bowl. Stir in the sour cream and continue to stir rapidly until a smooth frosting forms. Stir in the vanilla and salt.

Add a dollop of frosting on the top of each roll and spread as desired. Enjoy warm or at room temperature. Store leftover rolls in the refrigerator. Remove the lid and microwave 15 to 30 seconds before eating to take the chill off.

Amber Ale Apple Butter Swirl Bread

This sweet bread incorporates the toffee notes of an amber ale along with spiced apple butter. A thick slice begs to be paired with a hot cup of coffee on a peaceful morning. Once braided and in the pan, this loaf is meant to rest in the refrigerator overnight so that you can bake it in the morning in time to serve it for breakfast or brunch.

MAKES 1 LOAF (ABOUT 8 THICK SLICES)

540 grams (4½ cups) all-purpose flour

2¼ teaspoons (one ¼-ounce packet) active dry yeast

6 ounces (¾ cup) amber ale

¼ cup light brown sugar

2 teaspoons fine sea salt

8 tablespoons (1 stick) unsalted butter, very soft at room temperature

2 large eggs

¾ cup prepared apple butter

Egg wash

2 tablespoons granulated sugar

Add 120 grams (1 cup) of the flour to the bowl of a stand mixer fitted with the dough hook. Add the yeast and the beer. Stir it gently to combine. Let it sit for 30 minutes.

Add the remaining flour with the mixer on low, then add the sugar and salt. Scrape the sides of the bowl as needed. Mix in the butter until it's blended into the dough. Finally mix in the eggs. Increase the speed of the mixer. Let the mixer knead the dough for 10 minutes. It will be sticky and you will likely need to scrape the sides of the bowl occasionally.

After 10 minutes the dough should form a ball in the center of the mixer. It will be slightly tacky but it should pull away from your fingers when you pull it out of the bowl. Transfer the dough to a floured surface and knead it into a ball. Place it in a large bowl coated with butter. Cover and let it proof for 90 minutes, until it's nearly doubled in size.

Grease a 9-by-5-inch loaf pan with butter.

Punch down the dough and turn it out onto a well-floured surface. Use a rolling pin to roll it to a 14-by-20-inch rectangle. Spread the apple butter over the left half of the rectangle, leaving about a ½ inch around the top, bottom, and left edges.

Fold the right side of the dough over the side with the apple butter. Gently press the edges and roll the rolling pin over the new rectangle to smash the apple butter between the dough. Turn the rectangle so the long side faces you and roll up the dough, starting at the bottom, to form a tight log. Tuck in each end.

Find a Beer: Breckenridge Brewery Avalanche Amber Ale, Full Sail Brewing Company Full Sail Amber, New Belgium Brewing Fat Tire Belgian Style Ale

continued

Use a serrated knife to cut the log in half lengthwise. Place the two halves cut side up to expose the layers. Braid the two halves, keeping the cut side facing upward. Tuck the ends under and place the loaf in the prepared loaf pan.

Once the braided loaf is in the loaf pan, cover it with a buttered sheet of plastic wrap. Refrigerate it overnight, about 12 hours. Remove the loaf from the refrigerator at least 2 hours before baking and let it sit at room temperature.

Preheat the oven to 375°F. Brush the loaf with egg wash. Bake for 55 to 60 minutes, until the internal temperature reaches 190°F. Time may be influenced by the temperature of the room where the loaf rested before baking, so begin checking the loaf at 30 minutes. If the top appears to be turning too dark, cover it with a tent of aluminum foil to reduce further browning.

While it bakes, bring the granulated sugar and 2 tablespoons of water to a boil in a small saucepan over medium-high heat. Boil for 1 minute, until the syrup thickens slightly. Remove it from the heat.

Remove the bread from the oven and brush with the sugar syrup. Let it cool for 15 minutes. Run a knife along all of the edges. Either lift the bread out of the pan, or gently invert the pan onto a plate to release the bread. Let it cool 10 more minutes. Use a serrated knife to slice and serve warm or at room temperature.

Blueberry Beer Bagels

Fruit beers can be fiercely aromatic, especially when flavored with berries. As soon as you pour the beer into the mixer for these bagels, a berry scent will fill your kitchen. The dried blueberries will soften as the dough proofs and on the second kneading you'll see beautiful streaks of purple through your bagels as you shape them. These chewy beer bagels are best served soon after baking. I can easily eat one without any spread at all, but don't shy away from a thick layer of flavored cream cheese if you wish!

MAKES 8 BAGELS

480 grams (4 cups) all purpose flour

2¼ teaspoons (one ¼-ounce packet) active dry yeast

12 ounces (1½ cups) blueberry fruit ale, such as blueberry wheat

1 tablespoon granulated sugar

1 teaspoon fine sea salt

¼ cup dried blueberries

1 tablespoon brown sugar

1 tablespoon honey

Egg wash

Add the flour and yeast to the bowl of a stand mixer fitted with the dough hook. Turn the mixer to low and pour in the beer. Scrape the sides of the bowl as needed and mix until a dough begins to form. Mix in the granulated sugar and salt.

Allow the mixer to knead the dough for 1 minute. Add the dried blueberries. Let the mixer continue to knead the dough for 4 more minutes. Turn the dough ball out onto a floured surface and knead by hand for another 3 to 4 minutes until it's smooth and elastic. Transfer it to a bowl that has been greased with butter or cooking oil, cover it, and let it proof until it's doubled in size, 60 to 90 minutes.

Fill a large soup pot with about 4 inches of water. Add the brown sugar and honey. Just before the bagel dough is done proofing, bring the water to a boil over medium-high heat.

Preheat the oven to 425°F. Line two baking sheets with parchment paper. Punch down the dough. Knead it back into a ball and cut it into eight equal pieces, about 4 ounces each. Roll each into a ball and then poke a hole in the center of each ball. Gently pull the dough apart to form a bagel-shaped ring.

Work two to three at a time and carefully drop the bagels into the boiling water. Cook for 2 minutes, flip with a slotted spoon, and cook 1 more minute. Transfer the bagels to one of the prepared baking sheets. Continue until you have four bagels boiled.

Brush the bagels with egg wash. Bake for about 25 minutes, until they're golden brown and baked through the center. While the first batch of bagels bake, continue the rolling and boiling process with the remaining four bagels. Allow the bagels to cool 5 minutes before enjoying warm or at room temperature.

 **Find a Beer:** Abita Brewing Company Blueberry Wheat, Blue Point Brewing Company Blueberry Ale, Sea Dog Brewing Company Blueberry Wheat Ale

Cream Ale Irish Soda Bread

Historically, Irish Soda Bread was meant to be a simple recipe that could be baked every day using few ingredients. While more traditional loaves were flatter without the puffy look you commonly see today, what gives the bread a little rise without yeast is a reaction between an acid and baking soda. Traditionally, buttermilk was the source of acid, as it falls roughly between 4.5 and 5.0 on the pH scale (slightly acidic). It turns out that most beers also fall between 4.0 and 5.0, making it an easy substitution with the bonus of malty sweetness that makes the flavor of the bread more complex. I choose a cream ale here because one of my favorite beers from my travels is Kilkenny, an Irish cream ale. Any cream ale will work and those with hints of vanilla are especially good options.

MAKES 1 LOAF (10 TO 12 LARGE SLICES)

510 grams (4¼ cups) all-purpose flour
3 tablespoons sugar
1¼ teaspoons fine sea salt
1 teaspoon baking soda
4 tablespoons (½ stick) cold unsalted butter, cubed
12 ounces (1½ cups) cream ale
⅓ cup golden raisins or currants
¼ teaspoon pure vanilla extract

Preheat the oven to 400°F. Line a baking sheet with parchment paper.

Stir together the flour, sugar, salt, and baking soda in a large mixing bowl. Add the butter cubes and use a pastry blender or two knives to work the butter into the dough until it is evenly distributed in about pea-sized pieces.

Pour in the beer and stir just until combined. Add the raisins and vanilla. Stir to gently combine. At this point, you may need to switch to clean hands and knead the fruit into the bread. Be careful not to overwork the dough, though.

Transfer the dough to a floured surface and knead it into a ball. Place the dough on the baking sheet and use a serrated knife to cut a cross into the top of the dough.

Bake 48 to 50 minutes, until the bread is browned and the internal temperature reaches 175°F. Remove the bread from the oven and let it cool 10 minutes before slicing to serve.

Find a Beer: Anderson Valley Brewing Company Summer Solstice, New Glarus Brewing Company Spotted Cow, Sun King Brewing Company Sunlight Cream Ale

English Bitter English Muffins

If you have never made English muffins at home, you will quickly discover that the store-bought version can't hold a candle to homemade. Beer makes both the flavor and the texture even better. Don't be turned off by the beer name, English bitter. It is simply the name for a style that is essentially a pale ale. While the hoppy bitterness is often considered moderate, it is much less bitter than most pale ales in the United States. It's an ideal choice for the batter of a classic English muffin. You might need to seek out a growler from a small brewery experimenting with English styles for this one or hop over to the international section of your beer store. Once baked and cooled, split these muffins with a fork so that they maintain the small crevices throughout the interior. Then toast them and top with honey or a sweet spread like the Belgian Blonde Ale Beer Jelly (page 190).

MAKES 8 MUFFINS

270 grams (2¼ cups) bread flour
2¼ teaspoons (one ¼-ounce packet) active dry yeast
6 ounces (¾ cup) English bitter
½ teaspoon fine sea salt
1 tablespoon unsalted butter, softened at room temperature
1 tablespoon sugar
1 large egg
Semolina flour for the griddle

Add the flour and yeast to the bowl of a stand mixer fitted with the dough hook. Turn the mixer to low and pour in the beer. Scrape the sides of the bowl as needed and mix until a dough begins to form. Mix in the salt. Then add the butter and the sugar, and finally the egg. The dough will be very sticky. Depending on the size of your mixer, you might need to work the egg into the dough with a rubber spatula before returning it to the mixer to allow the dough hook to continue kneading.

Allow the mixer to knead the dough for 5 minutes. Use floured hands to work with the dough and turn it out onto a well-floured surface. Gently knead the dough by hand for 1 minute and form it into a smooth ball. Transfer it to a greased bowl. Cover it and let it proof for 90 minutes to 2 hours. It should puff up and nearly double in size.

Punch down the dough and transfer it to a floured surface. Cut the dough into eight pieces, about 2½ ounces each. Form each piece into a ball and then flatten into a disk about 3¼ inches in diameter.

Heat a well-seasoned or greased cast-iron griddle, or a nonstick griddle, over low heat. Sprinkle the surface with semolina flour. Cook the English muffins for 5 to 10 minutes on each side, until they're dark golden brown and no longer doughy in the center. Cool them before splitting and toasting to serve.

Find a Beer: Marshall Brewing Company McNellie's Pub Ale, Victory Brewing Company Uncle Teddy's Bitter, Redhook Ale Brewery Extra Special Bitter

White Chocolate Cherry Vanilla Ale Loaf

Serve this bread for breakfast or brunch, either on the side as a pastry or by toasting it to spread with creamy butter. The bread is rich and tender due to the butter and egg yolks mixed in. I make a suggestion for European-style butter here because of the similarities this bread has with a brioche. This type of butter has a higher fat content and tangier flavor that creates a rich and tender loaf. Choose a lightly colored beer infused with vanilla flavors. My favorite is a vanilla cream ale, but a vanilla blonde ale would work well, too. That vanilla combines with the white chocolate chips and dried cherries to make each thick slice a sweet treat.

MAKES 1 LOAF (ABOUT 8 THICK SLICES)

390 grams (3¼ cups) bread flour

2¼ teaspoons (one ¼-ounce packet) active dry yeast

6 ounces (¾ cup) vanilla-flavored ale, such as vanilla cream ale

¼ cup sugar

1½ teaspoons fine sea salt

8 tablespoons (1 stick) unsalted butter (preferably European-style), softened

3 large egg yolks

¼ teaspoon ground vanilla bean

½ cup sweetened dried cherries

½ cup white chocolate chips

Egg wash

Add the flour and yeast to the bowl of a stand mixer fitted with the dough hook. Turn it to low and pour in the beer. Scrape the sides of the bowl as needed and mix until a dough begins to form.

Mix in the sugar and salt. Add the butter and the egg yolks. Then add the vanilla bean.

Increase the speed of the mixer and allow it to knead the dough for 9 minutes. Scrape the bowl a few times as it kneads. Add the cherries and white chocolate chips and mix for 1 more minute. It will be heavy and sticky, but easy to handle and shape with floured hands.

Turn the dough out onto a floured surface and knead into a ball, working any loose mix-ins into the dough. Place the dough in a bowl that has been greased with butter. Cover it and let it proof in a draft-free spot for 2 hours. It will nearly double in size. Punch down the dough, cover it, and let it proof in the fridge for 2 hours. You can also leave it in overnight (8 hours) if you prefer to bake it in the morning. It will puff back up to nearly double in size.

Preheat the oven to 350°F. Grease a 9-by-5-inch loaf pan with butter.

Remove the dough from the refrigerator. It should be easy to work with, almost like a sugar cookie dough. Divide it in two and roll each half

Find a Beer: Blackhorse Brewery Vanilla Cream Ale, Garage Brewing Company Orange Vanilla Cream Ale, Mother Earth Brew Company Cali Creamin' Vanilla Cream Ale

continued

to about 12-inch logs. Twist the logs around each other, like you are braiding with two strands, and tuck the ends under, forming an oblong loaf. Place the loaf in the prepared pan and press it down gently. Brush it with egg wash. Place the pan on the stove and let it proof for 1 more hour. It should expand to touch all sides of the pan.

Brush the loaf with more egg wash. Bake it for 50 minutes, until the internal temperature reaches 190°F. After 30 minutes, if you feel the top is becoming too brown, place a tent of aluminum foil over the loaf for the remainder of the baking time.

Allow the loaf to sit until it's cool enough to handle, then remove it from the pan and slice to serve.

Savory Black Ale Coffee Cake with Mushrooms and Goat Cheese

This coffee cake is a great option when you want something savory for breakfast, but eggs and bacon aren't quite right. The base uses a rich and malty black ale, and, similar to a focaccia, deep indentations are made in the surface of the bread before baking. These shallow spots are filled with a tempting mix of sautéed mushrooms and onions along with tangy goat cheese. Once baked it is sliced into wedges and served warm.

SERVES 8

300 grams (2½ cups) all-purpose flour

2¼ teaspoons (one ¼-ounce packet) active dry yeast

6 ounces (¾ cup) black ale

1½ teaspoons fine sea salt

4 tablespoons extra virgin olive oil, plus extra to brush dough

1¼ teaspoons thyme leaves, plus extra for garnish

½ large yellow onion, sliced

8 ounces sliced white button mushrooms

¼ teaspoon ground black pepper

2 ounces goat cheese, crumbled

Find a Beer: The Duck-Rabbit Craft Brewery Hop Bunny ABA, Surly Brewing Company Damien Child of Darkness Ale, The Lagunitas Brewing Company Night Time Ale

Add the flour and yeast to the bowl of a stand mixer fitted with the dough hook. Turn the mixer to low and pour in the beer. Scrape the sides of the bowl as needed and mix until a dough begins to form. Mix in 1 teaspoon of salt and then 1½ tablespoons of olive oil. The dough will appear oily, but will come together as it kneads in the mixer. Mix in 1 teaspoon of thyme.

Allow the mixer to knead the dough for 5 minutes. Turn the dough out onto a lightly floured surface and knead it for 3 to 4 more minutes by hand, until it's smooth and elastic. Shape it into a ball. Place the ball of dough in a bowl that has been greased with olive oil. Cover it and let it proof until it's doubled in size, 60 to 90 minutes.

While the bread proofs, heat 2 tablespoons of the olive oil in a large skillet over medium heat. Add the onions and cook until they're browned, about 8 minutes. Add the mushrooms and the remaining ½ tablespoon of olive oil. Increase the heat to medium-high and cook until the mushrooms begin to darken and shrink, 5 minutes. Sprinkle in the remaining ½ teaspoon of salt, the black pepper, and ¼ teaspoon of thyme. Remove from the heat and let it cool.

Turn the proofed dough out onto a lightly floured surface and roll it into a 9-inch circle. Grease a 9-inch cake pan with olive oil. Place the dough

continued

in the cake pan. Cover. Preheat the oven to 375°F. Set the pan on the stove and let it proof for 30 minutes.

Punch down the dough in the pan, making four to five large indentations in the surface. Brush it with olive oil. Spread the mushrooms and onions over the dough, filling the indentations. Top with the goat cheese.

Bake 25 to 27 minutes until the surface begins to brown and the dough is baked through. Remove coffee cake from the oven, brush with more olive oil, and sprinkle with thyme leaves. Slice into eight wedges and serve warm.

Stout Breakfast Calzone

This recipe takes breakfast favorites and wraps them in a soft pizza dough made with a mildly bitter stout and its deep coffee-like flavors! It is a fun, savory recipe to add to a brunch and beer pairing. A coffee or Irish stout makes a good partner for serving, or try pairing it up with a brown ale.

SERVES 4

300 grams (2½ cups) all-purpose flour
2¼ teaspoons (one ¼-ounce packet) active dry yeast
6 ounces (¾ cup) stout
1 teaspoon fine sea salt
2 tablespoons extra virgin olive oil
Egg wash

FILLING

1 tablespoon unsalted butter
3 scallions, sliced
½ cup diced green bell pepper
½ cup diced red bell pepper
6 large eggs
½ teaspoon fine sea salt
¼ teaspoon ground black pepper
½ cup shredded medium Cheddar

Add the flour and yeast to the bowl of a stand mixer fitted with the dough hook. Turn the mixer to low and pour in the beer. Scrape the sides of the bowl as needed and mix until a dough begins to form. Mix in the salt and then the olive oil.

Increase the speed and allow the mixer to knead the dough for 5 minutes. Turn the dough out onto a lightly floured surface and knead it for 3 to 4 more minutes by hand, until it's smooth and elastic. Shape the dough into a ball. Place the ball of dough in a bowl that has been greased with olive oil. Cover it and let it proof until it's doubled in size, 60 to 90 minutes.

Make the filling while the bread proofs. Heat the butter in a medium skillet over medium-high heat. Add the scallions and peppers. Cook until they're softened, about 5 minutes. Remove the pan from the heat.

Whisk together the eggs, salt, and pepper in a medium bowl. Pour the eggs into the skillet and return it to medium-low heat. Cook, stirring often, until the eggs are soft but fully cooked, about 10 minutes. Set them aside to cool.

Preheat the oven to 375°F and cover a large baking sheet with parchment paper.

Punch down the dough and divide it into four portions. Form each into a ball and then press or roll into about a 6-inch circle.

Add one-quarter of the egg filling to the center of each circle of dough and sprinkle with one-quarter of the cheese. Fold one side of the dough over to create a half moon. Pinch and fold the edges together. Transfer all four to the baking sheet.

Brush the calzones well with egg wash. Use a sharp knife to cut three slits in the top of each calzone. Bake for 20 minutes, until the crust is golden brown. Serve warm.

Find a Beer: Bell's Brewery Kalamazoo Stout, Deschutes Brewery Obsidian Stout, Sierra Nevada Brewing Company Stout

Note: Frozen, cooked sausage links may be used. Simply allow them to thaw completely before wrapping them in the bread dough and baking.

Porter Pigs in a Blanket

These cute little breakfast bites wrap pork sausages in a simple, slightly sweetened bread dough made with a hearty porter. The dipping sauce is really what sends these over the top! It's a simple mix of pure maple syrup and porter that has been reduced down to a thick, smooth flavoring. The amount of dough here is small—maybe too small for a large electric stand mixer to knead well. For that reason, it may be necessary to mix the ingredients and knead the dough fully by hand.

SERVES 6 TO 8

150 grams (1¼ cups) all-purpose flour
2¼ teaspoons (one ¼-ounce packet) active dry yeast
3 ounces (6 tablespoons) porter
½ tablespoon sugar
1 tablespoon unsalted butter, melted
Pinch of fine sea salt
16 uncooked pork breakfast sausage links (see Note)
Egg wash

DIPPING SAUCE
3 ounces (6 tablespoons) porter
½ cup pure maple syrup

Find a Beer: Anchor Brewing Company Anchor Porter, Founders Brewing Company Robust Porter, Sierra Nevada Brewing Company Porter

Add the flour and yeast to the bowl of a stand mixer fitted with the dough hook. Turn the mixer to low and pour in the beer. Scrape the sides of the bowl as needed and mix until a dough begins to form. Mix in the sugar and then the butter, and finally the salt.

Allow the mixer to knead the dough for 5 minutes. Turn the dough ball out onto a floured surface and knead by hand for another 5 minutes, until it's smooth and elastic. Form it into a ball and transfer it to a bowl that has been greased with cooking oil. Cover it and let it proof until it's doubled in size, 60 to 90 minutes.

Cook the sausages in a medium nonstick skillet over medium-high heat until they are no longer pink, 5 to 7 minutes. Transfer them to a plate lined with paper towels to cool completely.

Preheat the oven to 400°F. Line a large, rimmed baking sheet with parchment paper. Punch down the dough and turn it out onto a smooth surface. Cut the dough into 16 pieces, about ½ ounce each. Roll each piece into a ball and then roll the ball into a rope about 8 inches long.

Wrap each rope of dough snuggly around a sausage link. Tuck the ends underneath the link and set all pigs in a blanket on the prepared baking sheet. Brush the top of each with egg wash. Bake for about 12 minutes, until the bread is golden brown.

While the pigs in a blanket bake, reduce the beer to make the sauce by pouring the 3 ounces (6 tablespoons) in a small saucepan. Heat the beer over medium heat to a boil, then reduce the heat to prevent any boil-overs. Let it continue at a low boil, stirring often, until it reduces to about ¼ ounce of thick syrup, about 7 minutes. Transfer the reduced beer to a small serving bowl and whisk in the maple syrup until combined.

Serve the pigs in a blanket warm with dipping sauce on the side.

Sausage and Onion Doppelbock Biscuits

These biscuits make a hearty morning meal all by themselves. A dark, malty German doppelbock complements the sweetness of the onions and helps make the biscuit dough both rich and tender. I like to use a lean turkey sausage, but any variety will work. Just be sure to drain the fat from pork sausages before folding the meat into the biscuit dough.

MAKES ABOUT 10 (3-INCH) BISCUITS

1 tablespoon extra virgin olive oil
¾ cup diced yellow onion
12 ounces (1½ cups) doppelbock
½ pound ground turkey sausage
480 grams (4 cups) all-purpose flour
3 teaspoons baking powder
1 teaspoon fine sea salt
½ pound (2 sticks) cold unsalted butter, cubed
Egg wash

Heat the olive oil in a small skillet over medium-high heat. Add the onion and reduce the heat to medium. Cook until the onions are browned, about 10 minutes. Add 1 ounce (2 tablespoons) of the beer, increase the heat slightly and cook, stirring, until most of the liquid has evaporated, about 1 minute. Transfer the onions and any remaining liquid to a medium bowl.

Add the sausage to the same skillet and return the heat to medium-high. Break up the sausage into tiny pieces with a spatula as it cooks. Cook until the meat is no longer pink, 6 to 7 minutes. Drain any grease if necessary and transfer the sausage to the bowl with the onions.

Preheat the oven to 425°F. Line a large baking sheet with parchment paper.

Add the flour to a large bowl and stir in the baking powder and salt. Add the butter and use a pastry blender or two knives to work the dough until the butter is evenly distributed in pea-sized pieces throughout the flour.

Pour in the remaining beer and stir well. It will appear dry. Add the cooked sausage and onions. Stir well to combine. The dough will be slightly sticky. Turn the dough out onto a well-floured surface. Dust the dough with flour as needed to handle it more easily.

Use a rolling pin to roll the dough to about a ¾-inch thickness, about an 8½-inch circle. Use a 3-inch biscuit cutter to cut out biscuits. Re-roll the dough and cut to get 10 biscuits total. Place the biscuits on the baking sheet. Bake for about 22 minutes, until they're golden brown. Best served warm.

Find a Beer: Bell's Brewery Consecrator Doppelbock Beer, Sprecher Brewing Company German-style Dopple Bock, Smuttynose Brewing Company S'muttonator

Chapter 4

RISING ROLLS
YEAST ROLLS FOR SIDES, SLIDERS, AND SNACKS

In this chapter craft beer is used to create yeast rolls of all kinds. There are rolls with herbs and grains to serve alongside your favorite soup or stew as well as those that make inventive slider buns. You will also find stuffed and pull-apart rolls with savory meats and creamy cheeses that you might be tempted to turn into a whole meal.

Kölsch and Dill Dinner Rolls

The dough for these rolls uses a light, crisp kölsch to pair with fresh, earthy dill. Both remind me of the foods and drinks we've enjoyed in Germany and Austria. These make a good side for grilled meat or fish, but they shine their brightest alongside a rustic potato soup. If you can't find a kölsch, try a simple lager, pilsner, or even a pale ale.

MAKES 6 ROLLS

240 grams (2 cups) all-purpose
    flour
2¼ teaspoons (one ¼-ounce packet)
    active dry yeast
6 ounces (¾ cup) kölsch
1½ tablespoons chopped fresh dill
½ teaspoon fine sea salt
¼ teaspoon onion powder
Egg wash
Dill sprigs for garnish

Add the flour and yeast to the bowl of a stand mixer fitted with a dough hook. Turn the mixer to low and pour in the beer. Scrape the sides of the bowl as needed. Increase the speed and allow a dough to form. Mix in the dill, salt, and onion powder.

Once a dough ball forms in the center of the bowl, allow the mixer to knead the dough for 5 minutes. Turn the dough out onto a floured surface and knead by hand for 4 minutes, until the dough is smooth and elastic. Form the dough into a ball and transfer it to a bowl that has been greased with cooking oil or butter. Cover the dough and let it proof to increase in size about 50 percent, 60 to 75 minutes.

Punch down the dough and cut it into six rolls, about 2½ ounces each. Roll these into balls and place them on a small baking sheet covered in parchment paper. Let them rise for 20 more minutes.

Preheat the oven to 375°F. Brush the rolls generously with egg wash. Lay a small sprig of dill on the top of each roll and press it down gently into the egg wash.

Bake for 20 minutes, until the rolls are golden brown. Serve warm or at room temperature.

Find a Beer: Ballast Point Brewing Company California Kölsch, Left Hand Brewing Company Travelin' Light, The St. Louis Brewery Schlafly Kölsch Ale

Pilsner Pepperoni Pull-Apart Rolls

These rolls are the ultimate snack, but I won't argue if you want to make them your whole meal. Pieces of white bread that have been made tender with a pilsner are baked in individual rolls layered with cheese and pepperoni. They are best served warm, so call all snackers into the kitchen soon after you remove them from the oven.

MAKES 8 ROLLS

360 grams (3 cups) all-purpose flour

2¼ teaspoons (one ¼-ounce packet) active dry yeast

6 ounces (¾ cup) pilsner

2 tablespoons unsalted butter, melted

1 large egg

1 teaspoon fine sea salt

2 scallions, green and white portion finely chopped

2½ ounces (about ¾ cup) sliced pepperoni, chopped

4 ounces (about ¾ cup) whole milk mozzarella, diced

Egg wash

2 tablespoons shredded Parmesan

Add the flour and yeast to the bowl of a stand mixer fitted with the dough hook. Turn the mixer to low and pour in the beer. Scrape the sides of the bowl as needed and mix until a dough begins to form. Mix in the butter, and then add the egg. Mix in the salt. Add the scallions.

Allow the mixer to knead the dough for 5 minutes. It will be sticky at first, due to the scallions; scrape the sides of the bowl as necessary. The dough will become firmer and elastic as it is kneaded.

Turn the dough ball out onto a floured surface and knead by hand for 5 more minutes, until the dough is smooth and elastic. Form the dough into a ball. Transfer the dough ball to a bowl that has been greased with olive oil, cover it, and let it proof until it's doubled in size, 60 to 90 minutes.

Punch down the dough and turn it out onto a smooth surface. Cut the dough into eight pieces, about 2¾ ounces each. Cut each piece into six small pieces. Roll these small pieces into balls. (They don't need to be perfect circles.)

Preheat the oven to 375°F. Grease eight slots in a 12-muffin tin with butter.

Add three mini balls of dough to each slot and press down. Top each with an equal amount of pepperoni and mozzarella.

Top each slot with three more pieces of dough and press down firmly to form the dough and fillings into the shape of the muffin tin.

Brush the top of each with egg wash, then sprinkle with the Parmesan.

Bake for 22 to 25 minutes, until the tops are golden brown and the internal temperature of the muffins reaches 190°F.

Remove the muffins from the oven and let them cool for 5 minutes before carefully removing each roll from the tin and serving warm.

Find a Beer: Firestone Walker Brewing Company Pivo Pilsner, Oskar Blues Brewery Mama's Little Yella Pils, Sixpoint Brewery The Crisp

Pale Ale Cheeseburger Snack Rolls

When these rolls bake, a small pocket is created that surrounds a rich and meaty mix of ground beef, Cheddar, onions, and pickles—everything I love on a burger. Pale ale creates a soft dough that holds the fillings in place while the top of the rolls get slightly crunchy. These are best served warm out of the oven when the cheese is still smooth and creamy.

MAKES 10 ROLLS

360 grams (3 cups) all-purpose flour

2¼ teaspoons (one ¼-ounce packet) active dry yeast

6 ounces (¾ cup) pale ale

2 tablespoons unsalted butter, melted

1 large egg

1¼ teaspoons fine sea salt

FILLING

½ pound lean ground beef

¼ teaspoon ground black pepper

¼ teaspoon garlic powder

3 tablespoons finely diced yellow onion

¼ cup finely diced dill pickles

3 ounces sharp Cheddar, shredded

Egg wash

1 tablespoon raw sesame seeds

Find a Beer: Boulevard Brewing Company Pale Ale, Sierra Nevada Brewing Company Pale Ale, Sweet Water Brewing Company 420 Extra Pale Ale

Add the flour and yeast to the bowl of a stand mixer fitted with the dough hook. Turn the mixer to low and pour in the beer. Scrape the sides of the bowl as needed and mix until a dough begins to form. Mix in the butter and then the egg, and finally 1 teaspoon of the salt.

Allow the mixer to knead the dough for 5 minutes. Turn the dough ball out onto a floured surface and knead by hand for another 5 minutes, until the dough is smooth and elastic. Form the dough into a ball and transfer it to a bowl that has been greased with butter or olive oil. Cover it and let it proof until it's doubled in size, 60 to 90 minutes.

While the dough proofs, cook the beef over medium-high heat until it's no longer pink, about 5 minutes. Break it into small pieces as it cooks. Transfer the beef to a plate covered in paper towels. Sprinkle it with the remaining ¼ teaspoon of salt, the pepper, and the garlic powder. Set it aside to cool completely.

Punch down the dough and turn it out onto a smooth surface. Cut it into 10 pieces, about 2¼ ounces each. Roll the dough pieces into balls and then flatten the balls using a rolling pin or by pressing with your hands to create a 3½-inch circle with each.

Top each circle with an equal amount of cooled ground beef, onions, pickles, and then cheese. Carefully wrap the dough around the ball and pinch to seal. Turn the roll seam side down and gently shape it back into a ball. Be careful not to work the dough much as the top of the roll will be thin and you want to avoid it splitting.

continued

Place the stuffed rolls on a large baking sheet covered in parchment. Preheat the oven to 375°F and let the rolls rise on the oven for another 5 minutes.

Brush each roll with egg wash and sprinkle with sesame seeds. Bake them for 20 minutes, until golden brown. Remove the rolls from the oven and let them cool for 5 minutes before serving warm.

Rosemary and Roasted Garlic Red Ale Rolls

These rolls are for everyone out there who loves the crunchy edges. I'm with you. Filling and shaping these savory rolls as you would a cinnamon roll changes the surface area to create nooks and crannies that brown nicely in the oven. It creates crunchy bites along with a tender interior that is brimming with rich butter and sweet roasted garlic. They have a malty flavor from the red ale and a fresh earthiness from rosemary.

MAKES 12 ROLLS

1 head garlic, top third removed
1 tablespoon extra virgin olive oil
270 grams (2¼ cups) all-purpose flour
2¼ teaspoons (one ¼-ounce packet) active dry yeast
6 ounces (¾ cup) red ale
4 tablespoons (½ stick) unsalted butter, melted
1 teaspoon chopped fresh rosemary leaves (about one 6-inch sprig)
1 teaspoon fine sea salt
Egg wash
1 tablespoon cold salted butter to finish the rolls

Place the garlic cut side up on a square of aluminum foil large enough to wrap the whole head. Pour the olive oil over the garlic and wrap tightly in the foil. Set it aside.

Add the flour and yeast to the bowl of a stand mixer fitted with the dough hook. Turn the mixer to low and pour in the beer. Scrape the sides of the bowl as needed and mix until a dough begins to form. Mix in 1 tablespoon of the melted butter, ½ teaspoon of the rosemary, and ½ teaspoon of the salt.

Allow the mixer to knead the dough for 5 minutes. Turn the dough ball out onto a floured surface and knead by hand for another 3 to 4 minutes, until the dough is smooth and elastic. Form it into a ball. Transfer it to a bowl that has been greased with butter or olive oil, cover it, and let it proof until it's doubled in size, 60 to 90 minutes.

While the dough proofs, place the garlic in the oven and preheat the oven to 375°F. Let the garlic roast for 45 minutes to 1 hour, until it's tender. Remove it and let it cool. Grease each slot in a 12-muffin tin with butter.

Punch down the dough and turn it out onto a smooth, lightly floured surface. Use a rolling pin to roll the dough into a 11-by-12-inch rectangle.

Squeeze the roasted garlic cloves out of the skins and into a small bowl. Add the remaining 3 tablespoons of melted butter and the remaining

continued

Find a Beer: Coronado Brewing Company Mermaid's Red, Full Sail Brewing Company Amber Ale, Karl Strauss Brewing Company Red Trolley Ale

½ teaspoon salt. Use a fork to mash all the ingredients. Allow the garlic mash to cool, and as it does it will turn into a paste.

Spread the garlic paste evenly over the rolled dough, leaving about ¼ inch on each edge. Sprinkle the dough with the remaining ½ teaspoon of chopped rosemary.

Starting from the long end, roll the dough into a long log. Place the log seam side down and tuck in each end. Use a serrated knife to cut the log into 12 rolls, each about 1-inch thick. Place each roll cut side up in the muffin pan and press down gently.

Cover the rolls and place them on the preheated stove to proof for 30 minutes. Brush each roll with egg wash.

Bake for 20 minutes, until the rolls are golden brown. Rub the top of each roll with the cold salted butter. These rolls are best served warm.

Whole Grain Irish Stout Rolls

These rolls are full of whole grains and hold up well for dipping in a comforting stew or a creamy tomato soup. The richness of the stout adds flavor and the use of wholemeal flour, a type of flour commonly used in Europe, gives them a hefty bite that will satisfy a hungry belly. True Irish stouts can be difficult to find around the United States due to the attention that coffee and chocolate stouts garner. If you have trouble finding one, substitute an unflavored American or English stout.

MAKES 6 ROLLS

193 grams (1¾ cups) wholemeal
    flour (see Note)
2¼ teaspoons (one ¼-ounce packet)
    active dry yeast
3 tablespoons old-fashioned oats
2 tablespoons oat bran
1 tablespoon flaxseed meal
6 ounces (¾ cup) Irish stout
1 teaspoon sugar
1 teaspoon fine sea salt
⅓ cup raw pumpkin seeds
Egg wash

Add the flour, yeast, oats, oat bran, and flaxseed meal to a large bowl. Pour in the beer and mix well until it's combined into a dough. Add the sugar and then the salt. Mix in 2 tablespoons of the pumpkin seeds.

The dough will be soft but can be kneaded by hand on a well-floured surface. Turn the dough out onto a floured surface and knead by hand for 5 minutes. Shape the dough into a ball and place it in a bowl coated in olive oil. Cover it and let it proof for 90 minutes. It should increase in size by about 50 percent.

Preheat the oven to 400°F and line a baking sheet with parchment paper.

Punch down the dough. Form the dough back into a ball and cut it into six rolls, about 2½ ounces each.

Roll the pieces into balls and place them on the baking sheet. Brush each with egg wash and then roll the top of each in the remaining pumpkin seeds. Place them back on the baking sheet and let them proof on the stove for 30 minutes.

Bake for about 17 minutes, until the rolls are browned and baked through.

Find a Beer: Flying Dog Brewery Pearl Necklace Chesapeake Stout, North Coast Brewing Company Old No. 38 Stout, Sun King Brewery Ring of Dingle Irish-style Stout

Note: Wholemeal flour is most easily found online in the United States from popular flour makers such as King Arthur Flour.

Dried Fig and Brown Ale Bacon Rolls

When a bread basket is passed around the table at a restaurant there is always one kind of roll tucked under the napkin that looks a little different than the plain white or wheat. It's usually studded with interesting bits, maybe dried fruit. It's always the first to disappear. These are that roll. Brown ale and dried golden figs give them a beautiful light brown color, and they are filled with bits of crispy bacon!

MAKES 6 ROLLS

2 slices thick-cut, uncured smoked bacon, chopped
6 dried golden California figs, stems removed and diced
1 tablespoon honey
270 grams (2¼ cups) all-purpose flour
2¼ teaspoons (one ¼-ounce packet) active dry yeast
6 ounces (¾ cup) brown ale
½ teaspoon fine sea salt
Egg wash

Cook the bacon pieces over medium-high heat, in a large skillet, until they are crisp and the fat begins to render, 5 to 6 minutes. Adjust the heat accordingly to avoid burning the bacon as it cooks. The goal is crisp, but not blackened. Stir in the figs and cook for 30 more seconds. Remove the skillet from the heat and let it sit for 1 minute. Stir in the honey and set it aside.

Add the flour and yeast to the bowl of a stand mixer fitted with a dough hook. With the mixer on low, pour in the beer. Scrape the sides of the bowl as needed. Increase the speed and allow the ingredients to form a dough. Mix in the salt. Add the cooled bacon, figs, and honey from the skillet.

Allow the mixer to knead the dough for 5 minutes. Turn the dough out onto a floured surface and knead by hand for 2 minutes, until the dough is smooth and elastic. Transfer the dough to a bowl that has been greased with cooking oil or butter. Cover it and let it proof about 1 hour, until it's almost doubled in size.

Punch down the dough, turn it out onto a clean surface, and knead it back into a ball. Cut it into six equal pieces, about 3¼ ounces each. Roll each into a small ball. Place the balls seam side down on a large baking sheet covered in parchment paper.

Preheat the oven to 375°F. Set the sheet pan on the stove and let the rolls proof for 15 more minutes. Brush generously with egg wash. Bake 20 minutes, until the rolls are golden brown. Serve warm or at room temperature.

Find a Beer: Avery Brewing Company Ellie's Brown, Big Sky Brewing Company Moose Drool Brown Ale, Real Ale Brewing Company Brewhouse Brown Ale

Pale Ale Pretzel Rolls with Smoked Sea Salt

What's a beer bread book without some form of pretzel? These small football-shaped rolls are made with pale ale and given a modern touch with smoked sea salt. My favorite types of smoked sea salt are bourbon smoked and oak smoked, but feel free to get creative with a version flavored with other spices, such as chile.

MAKES 12 ROLLS

510 grams (4¼ cups) all-purpose flour
2¼ teaspoons (one ¼-ounce packet) active dry yeast
12 ounces (1½ cups) pale ale
3 tablespoons unsalted butter, melted
½ teaspoon fine sea salt
Egg wash
2 tablespoons smoked sea salt

FOR THE BOIL
⅔ cup baking soda
1 tablespoon fine sea salt

Add the flour and yeast to the bowl of a stand mixer fitted with the dough hook. Turn the mixer to low and pour in the beer. Scrape the sides of the bowl as needed and mix until a dough begins to form. Mix in the melted butter and then the fine sea salt.

Allow the mixer to knead the dough for 5 minutes. Turn the dough ball out onto a floured surface and knead by hand for another 3 to 4 minutes, until the dough is smooth and elastic. Transfer the dough to a bowl that has been greased with butter or cooking oil, cover it, and let it proof until it's doubled in size, 60 to 90 minutes.

For the boil, fill a large soup pot with 10 cups of water, baking soda, and salt. Just before the pretzel dough is done proofing, bring the water to a boil over medium-high heat.

Preheat the oven to 450°F. Line a baking sheet with parchment paper.

Punch down the dough. Knead it back into a ball and cut it into 12 equal pieces, about 2½ ounces each. Roll each into a ball and then shape each ball into an oval shape.

Working a few rolls at a time, carefully drop them into the boiling water. Boil for 2 minutes on each side. Remove them with a slotted spoon and transfer them to the prepared baking sheet.

Brush each roll with egg wash and sprinkle with smoked sea salt. Use a sharp knife to score each roll with two slits. Bake 20 minutes, until the rolls are golden brown. Serve warm or at room temperature.

Find a Beer: Sierra Nevada Brewing Company Pale Ale, Oskar Blues Brewing Company Dale's Pale Ale, Kona Brewing Company Fire Rock Pale Ale

Tropical Wheat Hawaiian-Style Rolls

Homemade Hawaiian-style rolls often use pineapple juice to create that pillowy texture and hint of tropical sweetness we are familiar with from the store-bought version. This recipe incorporates a similar idea, but in the form of beer! A tropical flavored wheat beer creates a punch of flavor, giving the rolls their characteristic sweetness. I like to use a passion fruit wheat beer, but pineapple or guava are great choices, too.

MAKES 12 ROLLS

450 grams (3¾ cups) all-purpose flour

2¼ teaspoons (one ¼-ounce packet) active dry yeast

6 ounces (¾ cup) tropical wheat beer

⅓ cup sugar

4 tablespoons (½ stick) unsalted butter, melted

2 tablespoons powdered milk

2 large eggs

1 teaspoon fine sea salt

Egg wash

Add the flour and yeast to the bowl of a stand mixer fitted with the dough hook. Turn the mixer to low and pour in the beer. Scrape the sides of the bowl as needed and mix until a dough begins to form. Mix in the sugar and then the melted butter and milk powder. Mix in the eggs and then add the salt.

The dough will be sticky, so scrape the sides as needed with a rubber spatula. Allow the mixer to knead the dough for a full 15 minutes. At this point a dough ball will form in the middle of the bowl. The dough will still be sticky but will pull away from the bowl when encouraged.

Use floured hands to handle it and turn the dough ball out onto a floured surface. Knead by hand for about 30 more seconds and form the dough into a ball. Transfer the dough to a bowl that has been greased with butter or cooking oil. Cover it and let it proof until it's doubled in size, at least 2 hours. You want it to be nice and puffy.

Grease a 9-by-13-inch pan with butter. (I sometimes use a slightly shorter pan, 9-by-11 inches, so that the rolls bake closely together like store bought, but either is fine.)

Punch down the dough. Turn it back out onto a floured surface. Roll the dough back into a ball and cut it into 12 equal pieces, about 2½ ounces each. Roll the pieces into balls. Place the balls in the prepared pan.

Preheat the oven to 350°F. Set the baking dish on the stove and let the dough proof for 30 more minutes. Brush the rolls with egg wash and bake for 20 to 25 minutes, until they're golden brown and the center of the rolls reaches 190°F.

Find a Beer: Kona Brewing Company Wailua Wheat, Maui Brewing Company Pineapple Mana Wheat, SanTan Brewery Mr. Pineapple

Amber Ale Molasses Rye Dinner Rolls

These rolls have a subtle rye flavor that pairs well with the toffee notes of an amber ale and the sweetness of molasses. They make an ideal side for a dinner that involves ham, sausage, or sauerkraut, or use them as a base for Reuben-style sliders!

MAKES 6 ROLLS

206 grams (2 cups) medium rye flour
60 grams (½ cup) all-purpose flour
2¼ teaspoons (one ¼-ounce packet) active dry yeast
6 ounces (¾ cup) amber ale
1 tablespoon unsulphured molasses
½ teaspoon fine sea salt
Egg wash

Add the flours and yeast to the bowl of a stand mixer fitted with a dough hook. Pour in the beer with the mixer on low. Add the molasses and the salt. Increase the speed and allow the ingredients to blend into a dough. The dough will form a ball in the center of the bowl. Scrape the sides of the bowl as needed. Let the mixer knead the dough for 3 minutes. It will be slightly sticky.

Turn the dough out onto a floured surface and knead by hand for 5 minutes, until it's smooth and elastic. Form the dough into a ball and transfer it to a bowl that has been greased with cooking oil or butter. Cover it and let it proof until it's doubled in size, 90 minutes to 2 hours.

Punch down the dough, form it into a ball, and cut it into six rolls, about 2½ ounces each. Roll each piece into a ball and place them on a small baking sheet covered in parchment paper. Preheat the oven to 375°F and place the baking sheet on the stove. Let the rolls proof for about 1 hour. They should increase in size by about 25 percent.

Brush the rolls well with egg wash. Bake for 20 minutes, until they're golden brown.

Find a Beer: Breckenridge Brewery Avalanche Amber Ale, Full Sail Brewing Company Amber Ale, New Belgium Brewing Fat Tire

Golden Ale Raisin Pecan Rolls

These rolls taste great as a savory side, but they also have just enough sweetness to be perfect for breakfast when topped with your favorite honey or jam. The strong flavors of a Belgian golden ale (also called a Belgian pale ale) pair well with golden raisins, buttery pecans, and the touch of brown sugar. If you'd like less of a boozy flavor, consider an American golden ale that is light and crisp.

MAKES 8 ROLLS

270 grams (2¼ cups) all-purpose flour
2¼ teaspoons (one ¼-ounce packet) active dry yeast
6 ounces (¾ cup) golden ale
1 tablespoon light brown sugar
½ teaspoon fine sea salt
⅓ cup golden raisins
⅓ cup chopped pecans
Egg wash

Add the flour and yeast to the bowl of a stand mixer fitted with a dough hook. Turn the mixer to low and pour in the beer. Add the brown sugar and the salt. Increase the speed and allow the ingredients to blend into a dough. The dough will form a ball in the center of the bowl. Scrape the sides of the bowl as needed. Let the mixer knead the dough for 4 minutes. Add the raisins and pecans and knead in the mixer for 1 more minute.

Turn the dough out onto a floured surface and knead by hand for 3 to 4 minutes until it's smooth and elastic. Form the dough into a ball and transfer it to a bowl that has been greased with cooking oil or butter. Cover it and let it proof until nearly doubled in size, about 90 minutes.

Punch down the dough and cut it into eight pieces, about 2½ ounces each. Roll the pieces into balls and place them on a small baking sheet covered in parchment paper. Preheat the oven to 375°F. Set the tray on the stove and let it proof for 45 minutes; the balls should puff up, increasing in size by about 50 percent.

Brush the rolls generously with egg wash. Bake for 20 minutes, until they're golden brown.

Find a Beer: The Bruery Mischief, Cigar City Brewing Golden Ale, North Coast Brewing Company PranQster

Chapter 5

SLICE AND SERVE
YEAST BREADS FOR SANDWICHES AND SIDES

From classic breads for sandwiches to tender doughs studded with fruits and nuts, this chapter is full of beer bread options. The loaves range from sliceable sandwich loaves to those that are rustic and best torn into hearty hunks. Craft beer is infused into each loaf, creating hints of mysterious flavor and textures that give each their own delicious identity.

Pale Ale Sandwich Loaf

This classic white bread uses the bold flavor of a pale ale for a loaf that slices easily for your favorite sandwiches. It pairs well with all kinds of meats and cheeses as well as with grilled vegetables. Use it for cold sandwiches or heat up a sandwich press for a warm, filling panini.

MAKES 1 LOAF (8 TO 10 SLICES)

540 grams (4½ cups) all-purpose flour

2¼ teaspoons (one ¼-ounce packet) active dry yeast

12 ounces (1½ cups) pale ale

2 tablespoons sugar

2 tablespoons unsalted butter, softened and divided

1½ teaspoons fine sea salt

Add the flour and yeast to the bowl of a stand mixer fitted with the dough hook. Pour in the beer with the mixer on low. Scrape the sides of the bowl as needed. Mix in the sugar and then 1 tablespoon of the softened butter. Finally, mix in the salt.

Increase the speed and allow the mixer to knead the dough for 5 minutes. It will be slightly sticky but will pull away from your hands and the bowl when encouraged. Turn the dough out onto a floured surface and knead by hand for 3 to 4 more minutes, until the dough is smooth and elastic. Form it into a ball and place it in a bowl that has been greased with butter. Cover it and let it proof for 90 minutes, until nearly doubled in size.

Preheat the oven to 400°F. Grease a 9-by-5-inch loaf pan with butter.

Punch down the dough and then knead it into an oblong shape. Place the dough seam side down in the pan and press it down gently. Let it rise on top of the stove for 1 hour. The loaf will puff slightly to fill the pan and rise about to the line of the top of the pan.

Bake the loaf for 30 to 35 minutes, until the internal temperature reaches 180°F. Rub the top of the warm loaf generously with the remaining tablespoon of butter. Let the loaf rest in the pan until it's cool enough to handle. Invert the pan to remove the loaf and allow it to cool completely before slicing to serve.

Find a Beer: Boulevard Brewing Company Pale Ale, Sierra Nevada Brewing Company Pale Ale, Sweet Water Brewing Company 420 Extra Pale Ale

Honey Whole Wheat Blonde Bread

This soft whole wheat bread is great to have around whether you need a sandwich or a slice of toast. It's dense but soft, with hints of sweetness from the blonde ale and honey. If you can find a honey blonde ale, choose that, as it will only enhance the pleasant sweetness.

MAKES 1 LOAF (ABOUT 8 SLICES)

396 grams (3½ cups) white whole wheat flour

2¼ teaspoons (one ¼-ouce packet) active dry yeast

6 ounces (¾ cup) blonde ale

¼ cup honey

4 tablespoons (½ stick) unsalted butter, softened, plus additional cold butter to rub over the loaf

1 tablespoon powdered milk

1¼ teaspoons fine sea salt

Add the flour and yeast to the bowl of a stand mixer fitted with the dough hook. Pour in the beer with the mixer on low. Scrape the sides of the bowl as needed. Mix in the honey, the softened butter, the milk powder, and the salt.

Increase the speed of the mixer and allow it to knead the dough for 5 minutes. It will form a smooth ball in the center of the mixer. Turn the dough out onto a floured surface and knead it by hand for 3 to 4 more minutes, until it's smooth and elastic. Form it into a ball and place it in a bowl that has been greased with butter. Cover it and let it proof for 90 minutes; it should increase in size by about 50 percent.

Preheat the oven to 350°F. Grease an 8½-by-4½-inch loaf pan with butter.

Punch down the dough and then knead it into an oblong shape. Place the dough seam side down in the pan and press it down gently. Let it rise on the oven for 1 hour. The loaf will puff slightly to fill the pan and rise to about the top of the pan.

Bake the loaf for 45 minutes, until it reaches an internal temperature of 180°F. Remove it from the oven and rub it well with the cold butter. Let it sit until it's cool enough to handle. Invert the pan to remove the loaf and let it cool completely before slicing to serve.

Find a Beer: Firestone Walker Brewing Company 805 Blonde Ale, Ska Brewing Company True Blonde Ale, Big Sky Brewing Company Summer Honey

Seven Nut and Seed Scotch Ale Bread

This nutty, rustic loaf uses sweet, slightly heavy Scotch ale to balance the earthy flavors of the white whole wheat flour. The sponge—a mix of flour, yeast, and beer—sits for an hour before the dough is mixed and allows the flavors to blend. It bakes into a crusty bread that can be sliced to top with your favorite jam or casually torn for a filling chunk to dip in soups or stews. There are several ways to create a bit of steam in the oven that results in a crunchy crust. For this loaf, I use the simple method of spritzing the oven with a water bottle, so be sure to have one handy.

MAKES 1 LOAF (6 TO 8 SLICES)

SPONGE

113 grams (1 cup) white whole wheat flour

2¼ teaspoons (one ¼-ounce packet) active dry yeast

12 ounces (1½ cups) Scotch ale

DOUGH

310 grams (2¾ cups) white whole wheat flour

1 teaspoon fine sea salt

¼ cup chopped raw pecans

¼ cup dry-roasted, unsalted chopped pistachios

¼ cup raw pumpkin seeds

¼ cup chopped raw walnuts

¼ cup dry-roasted sunflower seeds

1 tablespoon black sesame seeds

1 tablespoon raw sesame seeds

Egg wash

Find a Beer: Great Divide Brewing Company Claymore Scotch Ale, Oskar Blues Brewing Company Old Chub, Pike Brewing Company Kilt Lifter

Stir together the sponge ingredients in the bowl of a stand mixer. Let it sit for 1 hour. It will look lumpy at first. As it sits it will smooth out, and after an hour will look slightly foamy on top.

Stir the sponge, then add the remaining flour and salt for the dough. Allow the dough hook of the mixer to knead the dough on low until a sticky ball forms in the center of the mixer. Then continue to knead on medium for 5 minutes.

Add all of the nuts and seeds. Mix for 30 seconds. Turn the dough out onto a floured surface and knead by hand for 3 minutes. Shape it into a ball and place it in a bowl that has been greased with cooking oil. Cover it and let it proof for 90 minutes, until nearly doubled in size.

Preheat the oven to 450°F. Place a pizza stone in the oven.

Punch down the dough. Knead it gently and shape it into an oval. Let it rest on a baking sheet for 1 hour. Remove the pizza stone from the oven. Place the loaf on the stone.

Brush the loaf generously with egg wash and then score the top of the loaf with three to five slits. Place the stone with the loaf in the oven. Spritz the oven a couple of times with water. Close the oven door.

Bake for 30 to 35 minutes, until browned and the internal temperature reaches 180°F. Serve warm or at room temperature.

Cream Ale Peanut Butter Sandwich Bread

This peanut butter bread bakes into a sandwich loaf that makes the ultimate peanut butter and jelly sandwiches! Or better yet, use it as a base for your next grilled peanut butter and banana sandwich. The slight sweetness of cream ale complements its deep nutty flavor. The final loaf has hints of peanut butter in each bite, making it a great partner for those classic sandwich fillings or a winning breakfast toast.

MAKES 1 LOAF (10 TO 12 SLICES)

300 grams (2½ cups) bread flour

141 grams (1¼ cups) white whole wheat flour

2¼ teaspoons (one ¼-ounce packet) active dry yeast

12 ounces (1½ cups) cream ale

½ teaspoon fine sea salt

⅓ cup creamy peanut butter

Peanut oil

Add the flours and yeast to the bowl of a stand mixer fitted with the dough hook. Turn the mixer to low and pour in the beer. Scrape the sides of the bowl as needed and mix until a dough begins to form. Add the salt and then the peanut butter. Let the mixer knead the dough for 10 minutes, until it is soft but smooth and elastic.

Turn the dough out onto a lightly floured surface and knead it into a ball. Place the ball of dough in a bowl that has been greased with peanut oil. Cover it and let it proof until it's light, fluffy, and nearly doubled in size, about 90 minutes.

Preheat the oven to 375°F. Grease a 9-by-5-inch loaf pan with peanut oil.

Punch down the dough and knead it into an oblong loaf. Place the loaf in the prepared pan and press it down gently to fill the pan. Let it proof in the pan on the preheating oven for 1 hour.

Score the top of the bread with three to four diagonal slits. Brush it with peanut oil. Bake for 30 minutes, until it reaches an internal temperature of 180°F.

Remove the loaf from the pan once it is cool enough to handle, after about 30 minutes. Let it cool completely before slicing to serve.

Find a Beer: Mother Earth Brew Company Cali Creamin' Vanilla Cream Ale, Newburgh Brewing Company Cream Ale, Sun King Brewing Company Sunlight Cream Ale

Cinnamon Raisin Walnut Brown Ale Bread

This bread bakes into a rustic round loaf with a crunchy exterior that is ideal to slice for toast, but easy to pull apart for a less formal presentation. The caramel, toasted notes of a brown ale work well with sweet raisins and crunchy walnuts. The hint of cinnamon gives it the flavors of a breakfast bread, but because it only has a hint of sweetness, it also makes a nice addition to a dinner. As with the Seven Nut and Seed Scotch Ale Bread (page 92), this loaf also starts with a sponge that rests for 1 hour, so plan ahead.

MAKES 1 LOAF (8 TO 10 SLICES)

SPONGE

120 grams (1 cup) all-purpose flour
2¼ teaspoons (one ¼-ounce packet) active dry yeast
12 ounces (1½ cups) brown ale

DOUGH

390 grams (3¼ cups) all-purpose flour
1 tablespoon honey
1 teaspoon fine sea salt
1 teaspoon ground cinnamon
½ cup raisins
½ cup chopped raw walnuts
Egg wash
½ tablespoon salted butter

 Find a Beer: Avery Brewing Company Ellie's Brown, Big Sky Brewing Company Moose Drool Brown Ale, Real Ale Brewing Company Brewhouse Brown Ale

Add the sponge ingredients to the bowl of a stand mixer fitted with the dough hook. Stir it a couple of times and let it sit for 1 hour. It will become light brown and foamy as it sits.

Add the remaining flour and turn the mixer to low. Scrape the sides of the bowl as needed. Add the honey, and then the salt and the cinnamon. Increase the mixer speed and allow it to knead the bread for 5 minutes. Add the raisins and walnuts and mix on low for 30 to 60 more seconds.

The dough may be slightly sticky, but it will pull away from the bowl and will be easy to handle when sprinkled with flour. Transfer the dough to a floured surface. Knead by hand for 3 minutes, working any mix-ins that may fall out back into the dough. Shape it into a ball.

Place the dough in a bowl that has been greased with butter. Cover it and let it proof for 90 minutes, until nearly doubled in size.

Punch down the dough and shape it back into a ball. Place the ball on a baking sheet set on the stove. Preheat the oven to 425°F and place a baking stone in the oven. Let the loaf proof for 1 more hour.

Carefully remove the stone from the oven and transfer the loaf to the stone. Brush it with egg wash and score the top of the loaf. Set the stone with the loaf in the oven and quickly spritz the interior of the oven with water. Bake for about 30 minutes, until the loaf is golden brown and the interior reaches 180°F.

Rub the outside of the warm loaf with salted butter. Once the loaf is cool enough to handle, transfer it to a cooling rack and let it cool completely before slicing to serve.

Cranberry Smoked Gouda Porter Pecan Bread

I will rarely turn down a bread that has fruit, nuts, and cheeses worked in. I think they make the best sandwiches, adding bits of flavor and texture to your choice of fillings. My first thought on this bread was that I would use blue cheese to complement the cranberries, toasty porter, and pecans, but then I started thinking about smoked Gouda. I knew it was the right choice the second I opened the oven to check on the bread—that smoky aroma filled the kitchen immediately. If you can find it, use a smoked porter for this bread, otherwise use a standard porter without added flavorings.

MAKES 1 LOAF (8 SLICES)

300 grams (2½ cups) all-purpose flour

2¼ teaspoons (one ¼-ounce packet) active dry yeast

6 ounces (¾ cup) porter

1 tablespoon sugar

1 teaspoon fine sea salt

½ cup dried cranberries

½ cup raw pecan halves

3 ounces smoked Gouda, diced small

Add the flour and yeast to the bowl of a stand mixer fitted with the dough hook. Turn the mixer to low and pour in the beer. Scrape the sides of the bowl as needed and mix until a dough begins to form. Mix in the sugar and then the salt. Let the mixer knead the dough for about 3 minutes, until it becomes smooth and elastic.

Add the cranberries, pecans, and Gouda. Allow the mixer to knead the dough for 2 more minutes. Increase the speed to help mix in the fruit and nuts. It may not all mix in and that is okay.

Turn the dough out onto a lightly floured surface, work any mix-ins that are loose in the bowl into the dough, and knead it for 3 to 4 more minutes. Shape it into a ball. Place the ball of dough in a bowl that has been greased with butter or cooking oil. Cover it and let it rise until it's doubled in size, 60 to 90 minutes.

Grease an 8½-by-4½-inch loaf pan with butter. Punch down the dough and knead it into a circle, then shape it into an oblong loaf. Place the loaf in the prepared pan. Preheat the oven to 400°F. Cover the loaf pan and let the dough proof on the stove for 20 minutes.

Remove the cover and bake the loaf for about 35 minutes, until it's dark golden brown and reaches an internal temperature of 175°F. Let it cool for 15 minutes before removing it from the pan. Allow it to cool completely before slicing to serve.

Find a Beer: Anchor Brewing Company Anchor Porter, Founders Brewing Company Robust Porter, Sierra Nevada Brewing Company Porter

Dubbel Caramelized Onion Bread

In this bread, the boozy sweetness of the Belgian dubbel blends well with the sweet caramelized onion. It's baked in a loaf pan, making it easy to slice. Use this bread as a base for your next avocado toast or for a gourmet grilled cheese!

MAKES 1 LOAF (8 SLICES)

1 tablespoon unsalted butter
½ large yellow onion, sliced
300 grams (2½ cups) all-purpose flour
2¼ teaspoons (one ¼-ounce packet) active dry yeast
6 ounces (¾ cup) Belgian dubbel
1 teaspoon fine sea salt

Melt the butter in a medium skillet over medium heat. Add the onions. Cook, stirring occasionally, until they are almost fully caramelized but not mushy, 25 to 30 minutes. Most of the onions will be soft, but others will still maintain a firm texture. Set them aside to cool.

Add the flour and yeast to the bowl of a stand mixer fitted with the dough hook. Turn the mixer to low and pour in the beer. Scrape the sides of the bowl as needed and mix until a dough begins to form. Mix in the salt. Add the onions and any oils from the pan. The moisture from the onions will bring the ingredients together to form a dough. Let the mixer knead the dough for 5 minutes.

Turn the dough out onto a lightly floured surface and knead it for 3 to 4 more minutes, until it becomes smooth and elastic. Shape it into a ball. Place the ball of dough in a bowl that has been greased with butter or olive oil. Cover it and let it rise until nearly doubled in size, 60 to 90 minutes.

Grease an 8½-by-4½-inch loaf pan with butter. Punch down the dough and knead it into a circle, then shape it into an oblong loaf. Place the loaf in the prepared pan.

Preheat the oven to 400°F. Cover the loaf pan with a piece of parchment paper and let the dough proof on the stove for 20 minutes.

Remove the cover and bake the loaf for about 35 minutes, until it's dark golden brown and reaches an internal temperature of 180°F. Let it sit until it's cool enough to handle, then remove it from the pan. Allow it to cool completely before slicing to serve. `

Find a Beer: Allagash Brewing Company Dubbel Ale, New Belgium Brewing Company Abbey, The Lost Abbey Lost and Found

Bière de Garde Braided Brioche

A bière de garde is a French beer style that has a malty, toasted flavor. You will likely come across it as a blonde or amber beer. Either works well in this bread, and its mild flavors are intensified as the outside of the loaf bakes into a dark, golden brown crust. In addition to a rich, buttery interior, my favorite thing about this brioche is how it comes together in a small braided round loaf. It's a great loaf for gift-giving!

SERVES ABOUT 6

390 grams (3¼ cups) bread flour
2¼ teaspoons (one ¼-ounce packet) active dry yeast
6 ounces (¾ cup) bière de garde
3 tablespoons sugar
1½ teaspoons fine sea salt
8 tablespoons (1 stick) unsalted butter (preferably European-style), softened
3 large egg yolks
Egg wash

Add the flour and yeast to the bowl of a stand mixer fitted with the dough hook. Turn the mixer to low and pour in the beer. Scrape the sides of the bowl as needed and mix until a dough begins to form. Mix in the sugar and salt. Add the butter and the egg yolks. Increase the speed of the mixer and let the mixer knead the dough for 10 minutes. It will be sticky, but easy to handle and shape with floured hands.

Turn the dough out onto a floured surface and knead it into a ball. Place the dough in a bowl that has been greased with butter. Cover it and let it proof in a draft-free spot for 2 hours. It will nearly double in size. Punch down the dough and form back into a ball. Return the dough to the bowl, cover it, and let it proof in the refrigerator for 2 more hours. You can also leave it in overnight, for 8 hours, if you prefer to bake it in the morning.

Preheat the oven to 350°F. Grease a 6-inch round cake pan with butter.

Remove the dough from the fridge. It should be easy to work with, almost like a sugar cookie dough. Divide it in two and roll each half into about a 10-inch log. Twist the logs around each other, like you are braiding with two strands, and tuck the ends under and in toward the center to form a circular loaf. Place the loaf in the prepared pan and place the pan on the stove.

Brush the loaf generously with egg wash. Let it proof for 1 hour. It should expand to touch all sides of the pan.

Brush the loaf with more egg wash. Bake it for 50 minutes, until the internal temperature reaches 190°F. After 20 minutes, if you feel the top is becoming too brown, place a tent of aluminum foil over the loaf for the remainder of the baking time.

Allow it to sit until it's cool enough to handle, then remove from the pan and slice to serve.

Find a Beer: Two Brothers Artisan Brewing Domaine Dupage, The Lost Abbey Farmhouse Lager, Sugar Creek Brewing Company Bière de Garde

IPA Cheddar Loaf

When I worked in a bread bakery we used to make a Cheddar bread. It baked into a soft round loaf and always had cheese that would seep beautifully out of the sides as it baked. That cheese would then brown and caramelize on the outside but leave pockets of solid Cheddar on the inside as it cooled. IPA and Cheddar have always been a favorite flavor pairing for me, so this is my re-creation of that memorable bread with a craft beer twist.

MAKES 1 LOAF (8 TO 10 SLICES)

480 grams (4 cups) all-purpose flour

2¼ teaspoons (one ¼-ounce packet) active dry yeast

12 ounces (1½ cups) IPA

1 teaspoon fine sea salt

½ teaspoon garlic powder

6 ounces mild Cheddar, cut into ¼-inch cubes

Egg wash

1 teaspoon raw sesame seeds

Add the flour and yeast to the bowl of a stand mixer fitted with the dough hook. Turn the mixer to low and pour in the beer. Scrape the sides of the bowl as needed and mix until a dough begins to form. Mix in the salt and garlic powder. Continue scraping the sides as needed, and let the mixer knead the dough for about 5 minutes. It will be soft and slightly sticky, but also smooth and elastic.

Add the cheese and mix on low for about 30 seconds. Turn the dough out onto a lightly floured surface and knead it another minute, working the cheese into the dough, but being careful not to break it up too much. You want the cubes to stay mostly whole.

Shape the dough into a ball. Place the ball of dough in a bowl that has been greased with butter or olive oil. Cover it and let it proof for 60 to 90 minutes, until nearly doubled in size.

Preheat the oven to 375°F. Line a baking sheet with a piece of parchment paper.

Punch down the dough and knead it back into a ball. Place the dough on the baking sheet and let it rise on the preheating oven for 30 minutes.

Brush the dough well with egg wash. Sprinkle it with sesame seeds. Bake for 35 to 40 minutes, until the internal temperature reaches 180°F.

Let it cool completely to enjoy chunks of Cheddar throughout each piece, but it is also delicious when served slightly warm.

Find a Beer: Avery Brewing Company Go Play IPA, Bear Republic Brewing Company Racer 5 IPA, Founders Brewing Company All Day IPA

Three-Olive Pilsner Loaf

No-knead breads feel downright revolutionary the first time you make one. Not just because they take little effort, but when baked in a Dutch oven they get that crusty golden exterior that seems impossible to achieve for a home-made bread. I assure you, it's not impossible. This loaf is made with a crisp pilsner and chopped olives. It's my go-to when I need something special for dipping in a seasonal soup. If you've never made no-knead bread before, just a heads-up that it proofs in the refrigerator for around 20 hours and then needs to rest at room temperature for about 90 minutes before baking.

MAKES 1 LOAF (10 TO 12 SLICES)

600 grams (5 cups) all-purpose flour

2¼ teaspoons (one ¼-ounce packet) active dry yeast

12 ounces (1½ cups) pilsner

1 teaspoon fine sea salt

¼ cup chopped black olives

¼ cup chopped green olives (preferably canned table olives)

¼ cup chopped Kalamata olives

Add the flour and yeast to the bowl of a stand mixer fitted with the dough hook. Turn the mixer to low and pour in the beer and 4 table-spoons of water. Scrape the sides of the bowl as needed and mix until a dough begins to form. Add the salt and then all of the olives.

Mix the dough for 30 seconds, just until the flour is incorporated, and all the ingredients form a sticky, misshapen dough.

Scrape the sides of the mixing bowl and transfer the dough to a bowl that has been greased with butter or cooking oil. Cover and refrigerate the dough for 20 to 24 hours.

Remove the dough from the refrigerator and uncover it. Let it sit at room temperature for 90 minutes to 2 hours to remove the chill before baking.

Meanwhile, preheat the oven to 450°F. Place a 5- or 6-quart Dutch oven, with the lid on, in the oven. It needs to heat for at least 30 minutes.

Remove the Dutch oven from the oven. Gently shape the dough as you scrape it from the bowl and transfer it to the Dutch oven. Place the lid over the top.

Bake for 30 minutes. Remove the lid and bake for 10 more minutes so that the crust becomes golden brown. It is ready when the internal tem-perature is 180°F and the crust is golden with some bubbling.

Let the bread cool in the Dutch oven for 10 minutes before removing. Serve warm or at room temperature.

Find a Beer: Firestone Walker Brewing Company Pivo Pilsner, Oskar Blues Brewery Mama's Little Yella Pils, Sixpoint Brewery The Crisp

Jalapeño Cheddar Mexican Lager Bread

This cheesy, crusty loaf will become your favorite for serving with a bowl of chili or for creating a turkey sandwich with a twist! As with the Three-Olive Pilsner Loaf (page 107), this is a no-knead bread that rests in the fridge for up to 24 hours and then bakes in a Dutch oven. It uses a smooth Mexican lager to balance the boldness of Cheddar and hot peppers. I often choose pickled jalapeños that are labeled "tamed" for a little less heat, but that is not a requirement. Make it as spicy as you would like!

MAKES 1 LOAF (8 TO 10 SLICES)

540 grams (4½ cups) all-purpose flour

2¼ teaspoons (one ¼-ounce packet) active dry yeast

12 ounces (1½ cups) Mexican lager

1 teaspoon fine sea salt

3 ounces medium Cheddar, shredded

½ cup pickled jalapeños, drained, but not dried

⅓ cup chopped fresh cilantro

Add the flour and yeast to the bowl of a stand mixer fitted with the dough hook. Turn the mixer to low and pour in the beer. Scrape the sides of the bowl as needed and mix until a dough begins to form. Add the salt. Next, add half of the cheese, the jalapeños, and the cilantro.

Mix for 30 seconds, just until all ingredients are blended and form a sticky, misshapen dough.

Scrape the sides of the mixing bowl and transfer the dough to a bowl that has been greased with olive oil. Cover and refrigerate the dough for 18 to 24 hours.

Remove the dough from the refrigerator and uncover. Let sit at room temperature for 90 minutes to 2 hours to remove the chill before baking.

Meanwhile, preheat the oven to 450°F. Place a 5- or 6-quart Dutch oven, with the lid on, in the oven. It needs to heat for at least 30 minutes.

Remove the Dutch oven from the oven. Gently shape the dough into an oblong loaf as you scrape it from the bowl. Transfer the loaf from the bowl to the Dutch oven. Use a sharp knife to cut a shallow groove lengthwise down the center of the loaf. Place the lid over the top.

Bake for 20 minutes. Remove the lid and sprinkle the remaining cheese in the center of the loaf, along the groove you scored. Bake for 15 more minutes so that the crust becomes golden brown and the cheese bubbles and browns. It is ready when the internal temperature is 180°F.

Let the bread cool in the Dutch oven for 10 minutes before removing. Serve warm or at room temperature.

 Find a Beer: Epic Brewing Los Locos Mexican-style Lager, Ska Brewing Company Mexican Logger, 21st Amendment El Sully

Note: Look for dry sun-dried tomatoes in a bag, as opposed to the oil-packed variety. Seasoned varieties are fine to use. If oil-packed is the only option, dry them well before adding them to the dough.

Sun-Dried Tomato and Swiss Saison Bread

If I had to choose a favorite ingredient combination for a bread, this would be it. Back in my bakery days, we used to bake an oblong loaf that was aromatic with Italian seasoning and slightly spicy from hot sauce, with bites of chewy sun-dried tomatoes and Swiss cheese throughout. I decided to re-create that here with a hint of peppery brightness from a saison.

MAKES 1 LOAF (6 TO 8 SLICES)

360 grams (3 cups) all-purpose flour

2¼ teaspoons (one ¼-ounce packet) active dry yeast

6 ounces (¾ cup) saison

1 teaspoon Italian seasoning

1 teaspoon fine sea salt

3 tablespoons extra virgin olive oil

1 tablespoon hot sauce

½ cup chopped sun-dried tomatoes (see Note)

4 ounces Swiss cheese, chopped or shredded

Egg wash

Add the flour and yeast to the bowl of a stand mixer fitted with the dough hook. Turn the mixer to low and pour in the beer. Scrape the sides of the bowl as needed and mix until a dough begins to form. Mix in the Italian seasoning and salt. Add the olive oil and then the hot sauce. Let the mixer knead the dough for 5 minutes, until it becomes smooth and elastic.

Add the sun-dried tomatoes and cheese. Continue to mix for about 1 minute, until the mix-ins are worked into the dough. Turn the dough out onto a floured surface and knead it by hand about 1 minute, forming it into a ball. Place the ball of dough in a bowl that has been greased with olive oil. Cover it and let it rise until nearly doubled in size, 60 to 90 minutes.

Preheat the oven to 375°F. Line a baking sheet with parchment paper.

Punch down the dough and then form it into an oblong loaf. Place the loaf on the baking sheet covered with parchment paper and let the bread proof on the preheated oven for 30 minutes. Brush the loaf with egg wash and score three slits in the top.

Bake for 40 to 45 minutes, until the loaf is golden brown and the internal temperature reaches 180°F. Serve warm or at room temperature.

Find a Beer: Brooklyn Brewery Sorachi Ace Saison, Door County Brewing Company Pastoral, North Coast Brewing Company Le Merle

Spiced Ale Fruited Holiday Bread

My holiday season is not complete without a bread that resembles those classic spiced holiday creations found throughout Europe. My favorite for a while now has been German *stollen,* and many of the loaves I create mimic it in design and flavor. This bread is no exception. A spiced holiday ale or winter lager hydrates the dried fruits, enhancing the seasonal flavors, and a dusting of sugars creates a crunchy crust for each slice.

MAKES 1 LOAF (8 TO 10 SLICES)

FRUITS

⅓ cup chopped dried apricots

⅓ cup dried cranberries

3 tablespoons diced candied orange peel

6 ounces (¾ cup) spiced ale

DOUGH

360 grams (3 cups) all-purpose flour

2¼ teaspoons (one ¼-ounce packet) active dry yeast

¼ cup sugar

½ teaspoon ground allspice

½ teaspoon ground ginger

½ teaspoon ground nutmeg

¼ teaspoon fine sea salt

4 tablespoons (½ stick) unsalted butter, softened

1 large egg

⅓ cup slivered almonds

TOPPING

2 tablespoons unsalted butter, melted

1 tablespoon granulated sugar

2 tablespoons sifted powdered sugar

Place the dried fruits in a small bowl and cover with the beer. Set them aside at room temperature while you prepare the dough.

Add the flour and yeast to the bowl of a mixer fitted with the dough hook. Turn the mixer to low and add the sugar, spices, and salt. Pour in the fruit with the beer used for soaking. Mix until a dough begins to form, scraping the sides of the bowl as needed.

Increase the speed of the mixer and add the butter and egg. Allow the mixer to knead the dough for 5 minutes.

Use floured hands to transfer the dough to a well-floured surface. It will be sticky. Sprinkle with the almonds and some flour. Knead gently by hand, working the almonds into the dough, for about 3 minutes. Continue to sprinkle with flour as needed. Form the dough into a ball and place it in a bowl that has been greased with butter. Cover it and let it proof for 60 to 90 minutes, until nearly doubled in size.

Form the dough into an oblong loaf. Preheat the oven to 375°F. Place the loaf on a sheet pan covered with parchment paper and let it proof for 60 more minutes. Bake for 45 to 50 minutes, until the internal temperature of the loaf reaches 190°F.

Remove the bread from the oven and, while the loaf is still hot, brush it generously with the melted butter. Sprinkle it well with the granulated sugar. Then dust it with powdered sugar. As it cools, you can carefully pick it up and turn it while sprinkling with more powdered sugar to cover the sides. Let it cool completely before slicing to serve.

 Find a Beer: Deschutes Brewery Jubelale, Revolution Brewing Fistmas Holiday Ale, 21st Amendment Brewery Fireside Chat

Pale Lager Matcha Bread

This soft, slightly sweet loaf gets its beautiful flavor and color from an Asian pale lager and matcha tea powder. My favorite way to serve it is to slice it thick, toast it until the edges are crunchy, and top it with butter and honey. It also makes an excellent French toast if you have a little more time in the morning. Asian-style lagers are often brewed with rice, and they are an experimental brew for some craft breweries in the United States. If you can't find one, an American light lager, a blonde ale, or a German helles make a good substitute.

MAKES 1 LOAF (8 TO 10 SLICES)

510 grams (4¼ cups) all-purpose flour

2¼ teaspoons (one ¼-ounce packet) active dry yeast

6 ounces (¾ cup) Asian-style lager

2 tablespoons matcha tea powder

¼ cup honey

¼ cup peanut oil

2 large eggs

½ teaspoon fine sea salt

Egg wash

1 tablespoon black sesame seeds

Add the flour and yeast to the bowl of a stand mixer fitted with the dough hook. Turn the mixer to low and pour in the beer. Scrape the sides of the bowl as needed and mix until a dough begins to form. Add the matcha powder. Then add the honey and peanut oil. Mix in the eggs and salt. Let the mixer knead the dough for 15 minutes, until it is soft but smooth and elastic.

Turn the dough out onto a lightly floured surface and knead it for about 2 minutes, then form it into a ball. Place the ball of dough in a bowl that has been greased with peanut oil. Cover it and let it proof for 2 hours, until nearly doubled in size.

Grease a 9-by-5-inch loaf pan with peanut oil. Punch down the dough and divide it into three equal pieces. Roll each piece into a rope about 12 inches long. Braid the ropes and tuck each end under. Place the loaf in the prepared pan. Cover it with a piece of parchment paper and let it rise for 1 hour.

Preheat the oven to 375°F. Brush the loaf with egg wash and sprinkle it with sesame seeds. Bake for 35 to 40 minutes, until the loaf reaches an internal temperature of 190°F. If the top appears to be browning too quickly, cover the loaf with a tent of foil about 20 minutes into its baking time.

When the bread is cool enough to handle, remove it from the pan and allow it to cool completely before slicing to serve.

Find a Beer: Firestone Walker Brewing Company Lager, Upslope Brewing Company Craft Lager, Yuengling Light Lager

Chapter 6

TOP IT
PIZZAS, FLATBREADS, AND CRACKERS

Beer and pizza have always been great culinary partners, but in these recipes that relationship is taken to a whole new level. Beer is used to make creative crusts and toppings for pizzas and flatbreads that will leave you craving more. In this chapter you will also find pita and crackers to make a base for your favorite dips and spreads.

Basic Beer Pizza Dough

This is my go-to recipe any time I want to make homemade pizza. Many types of beer work well here so don't be afraid to experiment. Pale ales, pilsners, IPAs, light lagers, wheats, and even fruit beers can make a delicious base for your pizza. The dough bakes into what can be classified as a traditional crust. Not too thick, not too thin, slightly puffy, and a little chewy. You can bake it on a pizza pan, on a stone, or put it on the grill.

MAKES ONE 14-INCH PIZZA CRUST

300 grams (2½ cups) all-purpose flour

2¼ teaspoons (one ¼-ounce packet) active dry yeast

6 ounces (¾ cup) beer

1 teaspoon fine sea salt

2 tablespoons extra virgin olive oil

Add the flour and yeast to the bowl of a stand mixer fitted with the dough hook. Turn the mixer to low and pour in the beer. Scrape the sides of the bowl as needed and mix until a dough begins to form. Mix in the salt and then the olive oil. Let the mixer knead the dough for 5 minutes, until it becomes a smooth ball in the middle of the mixer.

Turn the dough out onto a lightly floured surface and knead it for 3 to 4 more minutes, until it's smooth and elastic. Shape it into a ball. Place the ball of dough in a bowl that has been greased with olive oil. Cover it and let it rise until it's doubled in size, 60 to 90 minutes.

Transfer the dough to a flat surface, a pizza pan, or pizza stone. Roll or press it into a 14-inch circle. Add toppings and bake according to your pizza recipe, generally at 450°F for 15 to 20 minutes.

Find a Beer: Firestone Walker Brewing Company Lager, Cigar City Brewing Tampa-style Lager, Oskar Blues Brewing Company Mama's Lil Pils

Grilled Cherry and Prosciutto Fruit Ale Pizza

Grilling cherries brings out an unexpected caramel flavor that complements their sweet and sometimes tangy characteristics. In this pizza those flavors are enhanced by using a cherry fruit ale in the crust. Look for any type of cherry beer in a style that is on the lighter side, like a cherry wheat beer. If you can't find a cherry beer, ales infused with blackberry or raspberry work well, too. The prosciutto crisps up along the edges as the pizza is grilled, offering a salty, crunchy bite to go with the cherries, smooth crème fraîche, and the cheese. Crème fraîche can be found in most specialty cheese sections of supermarkets. The Mexican version, called crema, can easily be substituted.

SERVES 4

300 grams (2½ cups) all-purpose flour
2¼ teaspoons (one ¼-ounce packet) active dry yeast
6 ounces (¾ cup) cherry ale
1¼ teaspoons fine sea salt
2 tablespoons extra virgin olive oil

TOPPING
24 large fresh sweet cherries, pitted
Fine cornmeal or semolina flour as needed
Olive oil or other cooking oil for brushing
⅓ cup crème fraîche
4 garlic cloves, minced
¼ cup thinly sliced red onion
3 ounces prosciutto, chopped
4 ounces fresh mozzarella, shredded or chopped
¼ cup shaved Parmesan
Chopped cilantro or parsley for garnish

Add the flour and yeast to the bowl of a stand mixer fitted with the dough hook. Turn the mixer to low and pour in the beer. Scrape the sides of the bowl as needed and mix until a dough begins to form. Mix in 1 teaspoon of the salt and then the olive oil. Let the mixer knead the dough for 5 minutes, until it becomes a smooth ball of dough in the middle of the bowl.

Turn the dough out onto a lightly floured surface and knead it for 3 to 4 more minutes, until it's smooth and elastic. Shape it into a ball. Place the ball of dough in a bowl that has been greased with olive oil. Cover it and let it rise until it's doubled in size, 60 to 90 minutes.

While the bread proofs, heat the grill to 450°F and brush the grate with oil. Divide the cherries and slide them onto metal grilling skewers or soaked wooden skewers. Grill the cherries for about 3 minutes on each side, until grill marks form and the fruit softens. Slide the cherries onto a cutting board and set them aside to cool. Once they're cool, halve or roughly chop the cherries.

Punch down the dough and form it into a ball. Divide the ball into 4 equal portions. Roll or press each portion into about an 8-inch circle. Transfer the crusts to a baking sheet dusted with cornmeal or semolina flour. Brush the crusts with olive oil. Place the pizza crusts oiled side

continued

down on the grill for about 3 minutes, until they're seared and cooked about halfway through.

Brush the tops with oil. Dust the baking sheet with cornmeal again and remove the crusts from the grill, flipping them so that the grilled, seared side is up.

Stir together the crème fraîche, garlic, and the remaining ¼ teaspoon salt in a small dish. Spread an equal amount over each pizza. Top with red onion, prosciutto, grilled cherries, mozzarella, and Parmesan.

Use a large spatula or pizza peel to transfer the pizzas back to the grill. The undercooked side will be on the bottom. Cook for 5 to 7 more minutes until the crust is cooked through and the cheeses are bubbly and browned. Garnish with chopped fresh cilantro or parsley before serving.

Find a Beer: Founder's Brewing Company Rubaeus Raspberry Ale, New Glarus Brewing Company Wisconsin Belgian Red, Samuel Adams Cherry Wheat

Meatball Marinara Pizza with Spicy Amber Ale Honey

A restaurant in my hometown makes an incredible Detroit-style pizza that's topped with meatballs and finished with a spicy honey drizzle. I must have it every time I travel back, but to tide me over I created this version with a twist of malty sweetness from amber ale. Whether you use homemade meatballs or store-bought, be sure they are precooked and well chilled for easy slicing.

SERVES 6 TO 8

300 grams (2½ cups) bread flour

2¼ teaspoons (one ¼-ounce packet) active dry yeast

6 ounces (¾ cup) amber ale

1½ teaspoons fine sea salt

3 tablespoons extra virgin olive oil, plus extra for greasing

SAUCE AND TOPPINGS

1½ cups canned crushed tomatoes

5 ounces (½ cup plus 2 tablespoons) amber ale

1 garlic clove, grated

2 teaspoons sugar

1 teaspoon dried basil

½ teaspoon fine sea salt

¼ teaspoon ground black pepper

Six to eight (2-inch) meatballs, sliced thin

4 ounces fresh mozzarella, sliced

SPICY HONEY

2 tablespoons honey

1 ounce (2 tablespoons) amber ale

¼ teaspoon crushed red pepper

Add the flour and yeast to the bowl of a stand mixer fitted with the dough hook. Pour in the beer and 2 tablespoons of warm water and turn the mixer to low. Scrape the sides of the bowl as needed. Increase the mixer speed and add the salt and olive oil.

Allow the mixer to knead the dough for 8 minutes. It will be slightly sticky and wet, sticking to the bottom of the bowl as it mixes. Use floured hands to gather the dough and place it in a bowl that has been greased with olive oil. Cover it and let it proof for 2 hours, until it's doubled in size.

While the dough proofs, make the sauce. Stir together the tomatoes, beer, garlic, sugar, basil, salt, and pepper in a medium saucepan. Bring it to a simmer over medium-low heat and cook for 10 minutes. Stir occasionally, then begin to stir more often as it reaches the end of the cooking time, to prevent it from sticking to the bottom of the pan as it thickens. Set it aside to cool.

Next, make the spicy honey. Stir together the honey, beer, and red pepper in a small skillet. Warm it over low heat for 1 to 2 minutes. Set it aside to cool.

Grease a 9-by-13-inch pan with olive oil. Punch down the dough and then press the dough into the bottom of the pan. It may not reach the corners just yet, and that is okay. Brush the top with olive oil.

Preheat the oven to 500°F. Place the pan on the stove, cover it, and let it proof for 1 more hour.

continued

Press the dough back into the pan. It should reach the corners now. Prick a few holes in the dough with a fork. Layer the meatball slices over the dough, then top with cheese. Spoon the sauce over the toppings in thick rows, nearly covering the top.

Bake for 22 to 25 minutes, until the crust is browned on the edges and the cheese is bubbling and browned. Remove it from the oven. Let it sit for 5 minutes. Carefully remove the pizza from the pan using the help of large spatulas or a pizza peel and place it on a cutting board.

You can leave the crushed red pepper in the honey or strain it out for less spiciness. Drizzle the honey over the pizza before cutting it into squares, and serve any extra honey in a dish on the side.

Find a Beer: Alaskan Brewing Amber, Bell's Brewery Amber Ale, Full Sail Brewing Company Amber Ale

Salami, Pineapple, and Smoked Cheddar IPA Pizza

My husband and I lived in Brazil for a few years, and during that time an expat friend of mine told me about a snack she'd encountered often. It included juicy pineapple heated in a skillet, then covered with smoked provolone cheese so that it melted over the fruit, draping it with smoky deliciousness. That is the inspiration for this pizza. The crust is made with a hoppy, fruit-forward IPA. At first it might resemble a Hawaiian-style pizza, but swapping a smoked cheese for mozzarella makes a world of difference! Smoked provolone is more difficult for me to find than smoked Cheddar, so I typically choose the latter.

SERVES 2 TO 4

300 grams (2½ cups) all-purpose flour

2¼ teaspoons (one ¼-ounce packet) active dry yeast

6 ounces (¾ cup) IPA

1 teaspoon fine sea salt

2 tablespoons extra virgin olive oil

TOPPING

6 ounces smoked sharp Cheddar, shredded

4 ounces sliced salami

1 cup canned pineapple chunks or tidbits, drained and patted dry

Add the flour and yeast to the bowl of a stand mixer fitted with the dough hook. Turn the mixer to low and pour in the beer. Scrape the sides of the bowl as needed and mix until a dough begins to form. Mix in the salt and then the olive oil. Let the mixer knead the dough for 5 minutes, until it becomes a smooth ball in the middle of the mixer.

Turn the dough out onto a lightly floured surface and knead it for 3 to 4 more minutes, until it's smooth and elastic. Shape it into a ball. Place the ball of dough in a bowl that has been greased with olive oil. Cover it and let it rise until it's doubled in size, 60 to 90 minutes.

Preheat the oven to 450°F. Place a pizza stone in the oven.

Punch down the dough and divide it in two. Form each piece back into a ball. Roll or press each ball into an 8-inch circle. Lightly flour or sprinkle cornmeal on a pizza peel and place one of the crusts on the peel, making sure it doesn't stick. Top with one-quarter of the cheese, then half of the salami, half of the pineapple, and another one-quarter of the cheese.

Slide the pizza onto the pizza stone. If your stone is big enough, repeat for the other pizza and bake both pizzas together. If not, bake the pizzas separately.

Bake for 12 to 15 minutes, until the crust is golden brown and the cheese is bubbling and browned. Let the pizza cool 2 to 3 minutes before slicing to serve.

Find a Beer: Kona Brewing Company Hanalei IPA, Sierra Nevada Brewing Company Tropical Torpedo IPA, SweetWater Brewing Company Goin' Coastal IPA

Pesto Seafood Saison Pizza

When my husband and I travel to Washington State we frequent a restaurant that makes a pizza loaded with Pacific Coast seafood like salmon, scallops, and shrimp. The sweetness is balanced by prosciutto, olives, and pesto to create a pizza unlike any other. With that favorite pizza in mind, this creation uses a light and peppery saison for a tender pizza crust topped with shrimp and scallops. My goal when buying seafood is to look for the most sustainable options available, and in this case I have a good source for small salad shrimp and medium-sized scallops, so those are what I use. Feel free to use large shrimp, prawns, or any other high-quality seafood you are able to get in your area.

SERVES 4 TO 6

300 grams (2½ cups) all-purpose flour
2¼ teaspoons (one ¼-ounce packet) active dry yeast
6 ounces (¾ cup) saison
1 teaspoon fine sea salt
2 tablespoons extra virgin olive oil

TOPPING

1 tablespoon unsalted butter
1 cup small cooked salad shrimp, thawed if frozen
12 medium raw scallops, thawed if frozen, halved or chopped
⅓ cup prepared basil pesto
3 slices bacon, cooked and chopped
⅓ cup kalamata olives, halved
6 cherry or grape tomatoes, sliced
4 ounces fresh mozzarella, sliced or chopped
Shaved Parmesan for garnish
Chopped fresh basil for garnish

Find a Beer: Brooklyn Brewery Sorachi Ace Saison, Door County Brewing Company Pastoral, North Coast Brewing Company Le Merle

Add the flour and yeast to the bowl of a stand mixer fitted with the dough hook. Turn the mixer to low and pour in the beer. Scrape the sides of the bowl as needed and mix until a dough begins to form. Mix in the salt and then the olive oil. Let the mixer knead the dough for 5 minutes, until it becomes a smooth ball in the middle of the mixer.

Turn the dough out onto a lightly floured surface and knead it for 3 to 4 more minutes, until it's smooth and elastic. Shape it into a ball. Place the ball of dough in a bowl that has been greased with olive oil. Cover it and let it rise until it's doubled in size, 60 to 90 minutes.

While the dough proofs, melt the butter in a large skillet over medium heat. Add the shrimp and scallops and cook for about 2 minutes just until the scallops are barely cooked through and the shrimp are warmed. Remove them from the heat to cool.

Preheat the oven to 450°F. Transfer the dough to a pizza pan or a warmed pizza stone. Roll or press the dough into a 14-inch circle. Spread the pesto over the dough, leaving about a half-inch around the edges. Top the pizza with the bacon, shrimp, and scallops. Next add the olives and tomatoes. Finally add the mozzarella.

Bake for about 18 minutes, until the crust is golden brown and the cheese is melted and beginning to brown. Let it sit for 5 minutes. Garnish with Parmesan and basil, then slice to serve.

Black Ale BBQ Chicken and Drunken Kale Pizza

Barbecue chicken pizza has become one of my regular homemade meals. Over the years, I also created a vegetarian version using kale that is equally as enjoyable. This time around I combined the two and added the dark, roasted, malty flavor of an American black ale in both the crust and sauce. This recipe uses leftover rotisserie chicken, which prompted me to dedicate it to our pug, Dixie. You could never sneak a rotisserie chicken into the house without her heading toward the kitchen to help.

SERVES 4 TO 6

300 grams (2½ cups) all-purpose flour
2¼ teaspoons (one ¼-ounce packet) active dry yeast
9 ounces (1 cup plus 2 tablespoons) black ale
1¼ teaspoons fine sea salt
3 tablespoons extra virgin olive oil, plus extra for greasing

TOPPING
¼ large yellow onion, sliced
2 cups finely chopped kale leaves
¼ teaspoon crushed red pepper (optional)
1½ cups shredded cooked chicken
Semolina flour or cornmeal for baking
4 ounces sharp or medium Cheddar, shredded

Add the flour and yeast to the bowl of a stand mixer fitted with the dough hook. Turn the mixer to low and pour in 6 ounces (¾ cup) of the beer. Scrape the sides of the bowl as needed and mix until a dough begins to form. Mix in 1 teaspoon of the salt and then 2 tablespoons of the olive oil. Let the mixer knead the dough for 5 minutes, until it becomes a smooth ball in the middle of the mixer.

Turn the dough out onto a lightly floured surface and knead it for 3 to 4 more minutes, until it's smooth and elastic. Shape it into a ball. Place the ball of dough in a bowl that has been greased with olive oil. Cover it and let it rise until it's doubled in size, 60 to 90 minutes.

While the dough proofs, heat the remaining tablespoon of olive oil in a medium skillet over medium-high heat. Add the onions and cook until they begin to soften, 3 minutes. Add the kale, cook until it begins to wilt, about 1 minute, and then turn the heat to low. Pour in the remaining 3 ounces (6 tablespoons) of beer.

Gradually increase the heat to medium-low. Cook and stir until the beer evaporates and the kale is softened and bright green, 1 to 2 minutes. Stir in the remaining ¼ teaspoon of salt and the crushed red pepper, if using. Set it aside to cool.

Stir together all of the sauce ingredients in a medium saucepan. Bring it to a simmer over medium heat. Cook and stir until it begins to thicken, about 3 minutes. Set it aside to cool.

continued

SAUCE

⅓ cup ketchup

3 ounces (6 tablespoons) black ale

2 garlic cloves, grated

1 tablespoon unsulphured molasses

½ teaspoon fine sea salt

¼ teaspoon ground black pepper

¼ teaspoon smoked paprika

When the dough is ready, preheat the oven to 450°F. Grease a pizza pan or sheet pan with olive oil and sprinkle the pan lightly with semolina or cornmeal.

Remove the dough from the bowl and press it out into a rustic round or oval shape, about 12 by 14 inches. Transfer it to the baking pan. Prick holes in the top in several places with a fork.

Spread on the sauce, leaving only about ¼ inch around the edge of the crust. Top with the kale and onions, then the chicken, and finally the cheese. Bake for 15 to 20 minutes, until the crust is browned and the cheese is bubbly. Let it sit 2 to 3 minutes before slicing to serve.

Find a Beer: The Duck-Rabbit Craft Brewery Hop Bunny ABA, Surly Brewing Company Damien Child of Darkness Ale, The Lagunitas Brewing Company Night Time Ale

German Pilsner Rye Flatbread with Sausage and Beer Mustard Sauce

This flatbread comes about from my love of German beer and food. I owe Germany and Austria the credit for sparking my interest in the history and evolution of craft beer. The region also taught me about the culinary beauty of an authentic sausage with mustard and sauerkraut. The crust is light on rye so don't let it scare you off if you aren't a rye fan. A crisp German pilsner in both the crust and the mustard sauce adds a burst of classic beer flavor.

SERVES 4 TO 6

180 grams (1½ cups) all-purpose flour

103 grams (1 cup) medium rye flour

2¼ teaspoons (one ¼-ounce packet) active dry yeast

12 ounces (1½ cups) German pilsner

1 teaspoon fine sea salt

2 tablespoons extra virgin olive oil

TOPPING

1 pound bratwurst-style sausage (see Note)

2 tablespoons spicy brown mustard

1 teaspoon cornstarch

½ cup fresh sauerkraut, squeezed to drain (see Note)

4 ounces Swiss cheese, chopped or shredded

Add the flours and yeast to the bowl of a stand mixer fitted with the dough hook. Turn the mixer to low and pour in 6 ounces (¾ cup) of the beer. Scrape the sides of the bowl as needed and mix until a dough begins to form. Mix in the salt and then the olive oil. Let the mixer knead the dough for 5 minutes, until it becomes a smooth ball in the middle of the mixer.

Turn the dough out onto a lightly floured surface and knead it for 3 to 4 more minutes, until it's smooth and elastic. Shape it into a ball. Place the ball of dough in a bowl that has been greased with olive oil. Cover it and let it proof until it's doubled in size, 60 to 90 minutes.

While the dough proofs, brown the sausage in a large skillet over medium-high heat, until it's fully cooked, about 10 minutes. Transfer it to a plate lined with paper towels and let it cool.

Add the remaining 6 ounces (¾ cup) of beer to a medium saucepan. Heat the beer over medium heat, until it simmers. Simmer, stirring often, until it reduces by about half, about 10 minutes. Remove it from the heat and whisk in the mustard and cornstarch until smooth. Return it to medium-high heat and cook, stirring often, until the sauce thickens and coats the back of a spoon, 30 to 60 seconds. Set it aside to cool.

continued

Preheat the oven to 400°F and place a large baking sheet in the oven.

When the dough is ready, punch it down and transfer it to a piece of parchment paper. Roll it to an oval shape about 11-by-15 inches. Use a brush to spread the mustard sauce over the crust. Top with the sausage and then the sauerkraut. Add the cheese.

Carefully remove the baking sheet from the oven and slide the parchment paper with the pizza onto the hot pan. Bake for about 25 minutes, until the crust is browned on the edges and the cheese is bubbly. Let it cool 5 minutes before slicing to serve.

 Note: Bratwurst-seasoned loose, ground sausage can sometimes be difficult to find. If so, simply buy a pack of uncooked bratwurst and slide the meat out of the casing before cooking.

Choose a sauerkraut from the refrigerated section of the supermarket versus a canned version. Any of your favorite flavors will work. I prefer garlic and dill.

Find a Beer: Brooklyn Brewery Pilsner, Santa Fe Brewing Company Freestyle Pilsner, Sierra Nevada Brewing Company Nooner Pilsner

Curry Chickpea–Topped Lager Flatbread with Yogurt Tahini Sauce

Bread flour, yogurt, and lager come together to create a soft flatbread. It's my favorite recipe when I want a bread base that is more chewy than crunchy or fluffy. Once it slides off the grill, it's topped with a simple mix of smashed chickpeas with curry powder and lemon juice. Just before serving, give it a drizzle of yogurt tahini sauce. It is a fun party appetizer when cut into smaller squares and can be served warm or at room temperature. For a tasty twist, serve it with Gose Chutney (page 189) on the side.

SERVES 4 AS A MEAL, OR ABOUT 8 AS AN APPETIZER

300 grams (2½ cups) bread flour
6 ounces (¾ cup) lager
1½ teaspoons fine sea salt
3 tablespoons plain Greek yogurt
1 teaspoon lemon zest
1 teaspoon plus 1 tablespoon
   chopped fresh cilantro
Olive oil for grilling

TOPPING

One 15½-ounce can chickpeas,
   rinsed and drained
1 tablespoon fresh lemon juice
1 tablespoon extra virgin olive oil
2 teaspoons curry powder
5 cherry or grape tomatoes, chopped
Cilantro for garnish

YOGURT TAHINI SAUCE

3 tablespoons low-fat buttermilk
2 tablespoons plain Greek yogurt
1 teaspoon tahini
1 teaspoon chopped fresh cilantro
1 teaspoon minced red onion
¼ teaspoon fine sea salt

Add the flour and the beer to the bowl of a stand mixer fitted with the paddle attachment. Mix on low, scraping the sides of the bowl as needed. Mix in 1 teaspoon of the salt and then the yogurt. Next add the lemon zest and 1 teaspoon of the cilantro. Mix on medium until it comes together into a slightly sticky dough. Transfer the dough to a well-floured surface and knead it into a ball.

Preheat the grill to 450°F. Roll the dough into a 12-inch circle. Brush the top with olive oil. Use a well-floured surface to ensure you can transfer it to the grill. Place it on the grill, oiled side down, and cook for 3 to 4 minutes, until it's seared and browned. Brush the top with more oil before flipping and cooking it for 3 to 4 more minutes on the other side, until it's golden brown. Remove it from the grill.

Add the chickpeas, lemon juice, olive oil, curry powder, and the remaining ½ teaspoon of salt to a medium bowl. Mash it with a fork until the chickpeas are partially mashed and partially whole. This can also be done in a single-serve blender by using short pulses. Stir in the tablespoon of cilantro.

Top the flatbread with the chickpeas, pressing gently into the flatbread. Top with chopped tomatoes and garnish with more cilantro.

Stir together the yogurt tahini sauce ingredients in a small bowl until smooth. Drizzle the sauce over the flatbread just before serving or serve the sauce on the side.

Find a Beer: Cigar City Brewing Company Lager, Firestone Walker Brewing Company Lager, Upslope Brewing Company Craft Lager

Helles Flammkuchen (German Flatbread with Bacon)

A few years back my husband and I spent the holidays in Berlin. We hopped around to all of the Christmas markets and we often ordered *flammkuchen* from the food stalls. This simple flatbread is most often topped with crème fraîche, bacon, and onions. We had many versions during that trip and the main difference was the crust. Some were cracker thin and others thick and chewy. My favorites were thin but slightly chewy, so I came up with my own version using helles, a traditional German beer. If you can't find one, a pilsner works well, too.

SERVES 2 TO 4

300 grams (2½ cups) all-purpose flour
6 ounces (¾ cup) helles
½ teaspoon fine sea salt
1 tablespoon extra virgin olive oil

TOPPING
2 slices thick-cut, uncured bacon
3 tablespoons crème fraîche
¼ cup thinly sliced red onion
Fresh dill for garnish, roughly chopped

Preheat the oven to 450°F and place a pizza stone in the oven.

Add the flour and beer to the bowl of a mixer fitted with the paddle attachment. Turn the mixer to low and add the salt and then the olive oil. Increase the speed and mix until a dough forms. Transfer the dough to a floured surface and knead it into a ball. Let it rest while you prepare the bacon.

Trim any large pieces of fat from the ends of the bacon. You want the bacon to crisp as it bakes and not leave a lot of grease, so slice it thinly, focusing on the meatiest parts. Discard any excess fat.

Divide the dough in two and form each piece into a ball. Place each ball on a piece of parchment paper and roll it into an oval about 6 by 12 inches. Spread each with 1½ tablespoons crème fraîche. Top with an equal amount of bacon and red onions.

Remove the pizza stone from the oven and slide one of the pieces of parchment onto the stone with the flammkuchen. Bake for about 18 minutes, until the edges are golden brown and the crème fraîche bubbles and browns. About 5 minutes before it is done, I like to use a pizza peel to slide the flammkuchen off the parchment and directly onto the stone, so the bottom gets crispier. Repeat the baking process for the second flammkuchen. Garnish both with dill before serving.

 **Find a Beer:** Maui Brewing Company Bikini Blonde Lager, Uinta Brewing Fest, Victoria Brewing Company Helles Lager

Find a Beer: Avery Brewing Company White Rascal, Bell's Brewery Winter White Ale, Cigar City Brewing Company Florida Cracker

Marinated Summer Tomato Witbier Flatbread

The light flavor of a witbier with hints of citrus and coriander always makes me think of summer and the best of the season's produce. Here, colorful heirloom cherry and grape tomatoes are marinated in a small amount of beer and spices. Then they are served over a flavorful flatbread crust that has been grilled until golden brown. Garnish this one with any of your favorite herbs. I usually choose cilantro or basil, but parsley and chives work well, too.

SERVES 4 AS A MEAL, ABOUT 8 AS AN APPETIZER

300 grams (2½ cups) all-purpose flour
2¼ teaspoons (one ¼-ounce packet) active dry yeast
5½ ounces (½ cup plus 1 tablespoon) witbier or white ale
1 teaspoon fine sea salt
½ teaspoon garlic powder
¼ teaspoon ground coriander
4 tablespoons extra virgin olive oil
Olive oil for grilling
⅓ cup shaved Parmesan
Chopped herbs for garnish

TOMATOES
1 pint mixed heirloom cherry or grape tomatoes, sliced
¼ cup finely chopped red onion or shallot
½ ounce (1 tablespoon) witbier or white ale
½ tablespoon extra virgin olive oil
½ teaspoon fine sea salt
¼ teaspoon ground coriander
¼ teaspoon ground black pepper

For the flatbread dough, add the flour and yeast to the bowl of a stand mixer fitted with the dough hook. Turn the mixer to low and pour in the beer. Scrape the sides of the bowl as needed and mix until a dough begins to form. Mix in the salt, garlic powder, and coriander, and then the olive oil. Let the mixer knead the dough for 5 minutes, until it becomes a smooth ball in the middle of the mixer.

Turn the dough out onto a lightly floured surface and knead it for 2 to 3 more minutes, until it's smooth and elastic. Shape it into a ball. Place the ball of dough in a bowl that has been greased with olive oil. Cover it and let it proof until nearly doubled in size, 60 to 90 minutes.

Meanwhile, stir together all the ingredients for the tomatoes in a medium bowl. Let it sit at room temperature while the dough proofs.

Heat the grill to 400°F. Punch down the dough and divide it in two. Knead each piece back into a ball. Roll each ball into a thin oval shape about 8 by 12 inches on a well-floured surface.

Brush the grill with oil. Place the flatbread on the grill and cook for 3 to 4 minutes, until it's seared and golden brown on the underside. Use the spatula to pierce any large air bubbles that puff up while grilling. Brush the top of the flatbreads with oil and flip them. Cook for 3 to 4 more minutes, until they're golden brown and cooked through.

About 1 minute before the flatbreads are ready to come off the grill, brush them well with olive oil. Drain the tomatoes and onions and arrange the slices over each flat bread. Leave them on the grill for about 1 minute, to gently warm them. Remove the flatbreads from the grill and top each with an equal amount of Parmesan and chopped herbs. Slice and serve them right away.

Wine Barrel–Aged Grape and Rosemary Focaccia

This focaccia has an intriguing mix of sweet and savory flavors. It is a tasty addition to a charcuterie and cheese board, or can be served as a side for brunch. Any type of beer that has been influenced by wine will work well. For example, some beers are aged in wine barrels while others are made with grape must or blended with wines. Just be sure to choose a golden variety versus a dark beer.

MAKES 1 LOAF (12 SLICES)

300 grams (2½ cups) bread flour

2¼ teaspoon (one ¼-ounce packet) active dry yeast

6 ounces (¾ cup) wine barrel–aged beer or beer made with grape must

1 tablespoon chopped fresh rosemary

1 teaspoon fine sea salt

1 tablespoon honey

2 tablespoons extra virgin olive oil, plus extra for brushing

1 cup purple seedless grapes, rinsed and dried

2 tablespoons shaved Parmesan

Add the flour and yeast to the bowl of a stand mixer fitted with the dough hook. Turn the mixer to low and pour in the beer. Scrape the sides of the bowl as needed and mix until a dough begins to form. Mix in the rosemary and then the salt. Next, mix in the honey and finally the olive oil. Let the mixer knead the dough for 5 minutes, until it becomes a smooth ball in the middle of the mixer.

Turn the dough out onto a lightly floured surface and knead it for 3 to 4 more minutes, until it's smooth and elastic. Shape it into a ball. Place the ball of dough in a bowl that has been greased with olive oil. Cover it and let it proof for 90 minutes. It will increase in size about 25 percent and will hold indentations when you press your finger into the dough.

Preheat the oven to 425°F. Transfer the dough to a quarter baking sheet (or a 9-by-13-inch baking dish) that has been sprayed with nonstick cooking spray (I prefer this over oils so that the dough will spread when pressed into the pan). Press and spread the dough until it covers the bottom of the pan. Cover it with a piece of parchment paper and let it rise for 30 minutes.

Press indentations into the surface of the dough with your fingers in several spots. Then press the grapes into the surface of the dough. Brush the dough with olive oil. Sprinkle on the Parmesan. Bake for 15 minutes, until it's golden brown.

Brush with more olive oil when you remove it from the oven. Let it cool for 5 minutes. The grapes may pop a bit and shrink back as it cools. Cut it into 12 pieces and serve.

Find a Beer: Dogfish Head Craft Brewery Mixed Media, Uinta Brewing Farmside Saison, Two Roads Brewing Company Sauvignon Blanc Gose

Grilled Beer Pita

This grilled pita is lighter and fluffier than what you might be used to from the supermarket, and that is why I like it. It has a chewy soft center and a surface made crisp from the grill. It's my favorite type of bread to dip in a smooth hummus or in a tangy olive tapenade. A number of beer styles work perfectly in this bread. I often turn to a hefeweizen or wheat beer, but pilsner, pale ales, and light lagers work great, too.

SERVES 8

480 grams (4 cups) bread flour
2¼ teaspoons (one ¼-ounce packet) active dry yeast
12 ounces (1½ cups) beer
2 teaspoons fine sea salt, plus extra for sprinkling
1 tablespoon honey
2 tablespoons extra virgin olive oil, plus extra for brushing
Vegetable oil for the grill

Add the flour and yeast to the bowl of a stand mixer fitted with the dough hook. Turn the mixer to low and pour in the beer. Scrape the sides of the bowl as needed and mix until a dough begins to form. Mix in the salt, then the honey, and finally the olive oil. Let the mixer knead the dough for 10 minutes, until it becomes a smooth but sticky ball of dough in the middle of the bowl.

Use floured hands to transfer the dough to a bowl that has been greased with olive oil. Cover it and let it proof for 1 hour. It will increase in size about 25 percent.

Sprinkle a flat surface with flour. Transfer the dough to the surface and divide the dough into 8 portions. It will be sticky, which is why I don't suggest weighing it. Just estimate equal pieces and use floured hands. Roll each piece into a ball. Sprinkle the tops with a little more flour, then cover them with a piece of parchment paper and let them proof for 30 more minutes.

Heat the grill to 425°F. Brush the grill with vegetable oil. Stretch or roll each pita to about a 6-inch circle. Place the pitas on the grill. Grill for 2 to 3 minutes on each side, until they're browned and baked through.

Brush the pitas with olive oil while they're still warm and sprinkle with more salt, if desired. Serve warm.

Find a Beer: Bell's Brewery Oberon Ale, Kona Brewing Company Fire Rock Pale Ale, Sierra Nevada Brewing Company Kellerweis

Sesame Flatbread Beer Crackers

I like to make these easy crackers with a crisp pilsner, but many beers can be substituted. Feel free to try a pale ale or light lager, too. I use a pizza stone to help get the crackers nice and crisp. You can allow these crackers to cool and then break them apart to serve, but I like to use a knife to cut them while they are still a little warm for slightly cleaner edges. They pair deliciously with the Classic Kentucky Beer Cheese (page 182).

SERVES 6 TO 8

210 grams (1¾ cups) all-purpose flour
2 tablespoons white sesame seeds
1 tablespoon black sesame seeds
¾ teaspoon fine sea salt, plus extra for sprinkling
½ teaspoon baking powder
6 ounces (¾ cup) pilsner
1 tablespoon extra virgin olive oil
Toasted sesame oil

Preheat the oven to 425°F and place a pizza stone in the oven.

Combine the flour, sesame seeds, salt, and baking powder in a large bowl. Pour in the beer and then the olive oil and stir well. Stir or gently knead the dough together into a ball. Divide the ball in three pieces.

Place a large piece of parchment paper on a flat surface. Roll a piece of the dough to about a 10-inch circle on the parchment paper. Transfer the paper to the stone and bake for about 15 minutes, until the edges are browned and the cracker is firm. After 5 minutes of baking, use a pizza peel or spatula to slide the cracker from the parchment directly onto the stone to finish baking.

Remove the cracker from the oven, brush with sesame oil and sprinkle with sea salt. Repeat with the remaining crackers.

To break the crackers apart, allow them to cool completely and then break them into similarly sized pieces. To cut, let them cool for 5 minutes before transferring them to a cutting board to cut into pieces.

Store in an airtight container until they're ready to serve, up to one day.

 **Find a Beer:** Bell's Brewing Lager of the Lakes, Odell Brewing Company 5 Barrel Pale Ale, Sierra Nevada Brewing Company Nooner Pilsner

Chapter 7

STIR AND BAKE
CRAFT BEER QUICK BREADS

When you want something freshly baked but lack the time for dough to rise, quick breads are the answer. Made with batters versus doughs, they use leavening ingredients like baking soda, baking powder, and acids to get their rise. Beer is a flavorful ingredient in these breads, which range from savory slices to sweet breads that can be eaten as a breakfast pastry or served for dessert.

Classic Beer Bread

This is the bread that most people think of when they hear the term "beer bread." A short list of ingredients comes together to create a sliceable loaf that is biscuit-like in texture. The typical beer choice for a bread that isn't overpowering with beer flavor is an American light lager. To make things easy and to keep ingredients minimal, I've followed suit for classic recipes and used self-rising flour. This bread is an easy, go-to recipe when you want to serve something from the oven that doesn't take all afternoon to make.

MAKES 1 LOAF (8 TO 10 SLICES)

339 grams (3 cups) self-rising flour

2 tablespoons unsalted butter, melted

1 tablespoon sugar

12 ounces (1½ cups) American light lager

½ tablespoon salted butter

Preheat the oven to 375°F. Grease a 9-by-5-inch loaf pan with butter.

Stir together the flour and butter in a large bowl. Add the sugar and then stir in the beer. Continue stirring until all the flour is hydrated and a thick batter forms. Pour the batter into the loaf pan.

Bake the bread for 30 to 35 minutes, until a toothpick inserted in the center comes out clean. Rub the top of the warm loaf with salted butter. Let it cool for 30 minutes before inverting the pan to release the loaf. Slice to serve.

 **Find a Beer:** Firestone Walker Brewing Company Lager, Upslope Brewing Company Craft Lager, Yuengling Light Lager

Cheese and Herb Pale Ale Bread

This recipe takes classic beer bread and adds a stronger punch of beer flavor with a pale ale. Then it's loaded with cheese that turns golden brown when baked. Garlic and dill mixed into the batter, along with less sugar than the Classic Beer Bread recipe (page 150), makes it a savory side dish perfect to pair with soup.

MAKES 1 LOAF (8 SLICES)

339 grams (3 cups) self-rising flour

2 tablespoons unsalted butter, melted

1 teaspoon sugar

1 garlic clove, grated

1 tablespoon chopped fresh dill

3 ounces medium Cheddar, shredded

3 ounces Monterey jack, shredded

12 ounces (1½ cups) pale ale

Preheat the oven to 375°F. Grease an 8½-by-4½-inch loaf pan with butter.

Stir together the flour and butter in a large bowl. Add the sugar, garlic, and dill. Add half of each type of cheese and toss to coat them with the other ingredients. Pour in the beer. Stir until all the flour is hydrated and a thick batter forms.

Pour the batter into the loaf pan. Top the loaf with the remaining cheese. Place the loaf pan on a baking sheet in case any cheese bakes over the side.

Bake the bread for 30 to 35 minutes, until a toothpick inserted in the center comes out clean. At about 20 minutes, if the cheese looks like it is getting too brown, carefully cover the loaf with a tented piece of aluminum foil for the remainder of the baking time.

Let it cool for 30 minutes before inverting the pan to release the loaf. Slice to serve.

Find a Beer: Kona Brewing Company Fire Rock Pale Ale, Oskar Blues Brewing Company Dale's Pale Ale, Sierra Nevada Brewing Company Pale Ale

American Wheat Sautéed Sweet Corn and Pepper Bread

I like a heartier cornbread that mixes in fresh corn and other seasonal ingredients. When I decided to make one with the bright flavors of an American wheat beer, I knew it needed a twist of texture and some add-ins that would pair well with the beer. One of my favorite summer side dishes is sautéed corn and peppers, and this recipe is inspired by that, but in beer bread form. Serve it at your next cookout alongside some smoky barbecue and creamy coleslaw.

MAKES 8 TO 10 SERVINGS

VEGETABLES

½ tablespoon unsalted butter

⅓ cup chopped mixed sweet or spicy peppers

⅓ cup fresh corn kernels (about 1 ear)

CORNBREAD

123 grams (¾ cup) medium or coarse ground cornmeal (see Note)

90 grams (¾ cup) all-purpose flour

1 tablespoon sugar

2 teaspoons baking powder

½ teaspoon fine sea salt

¼ teaspoon ground black pepper

2 tablespoons unsalted butter, melted

1 large egg

6 ounces (¾ cup) wheat beer

Prepare the vegetables by melting the butter in a medium skillet over medium-high heat. Add the peppers and the corn and cook until they begin to soften, about 5 minutes. Set them aside to cool.

Preheat the oven to 375°F. Grease an 8½-by-4½-inch loaf pan with butter.

Stir together the cornmeal, flour, sugar, baking powder, salt, and pepper in a large bowl. Toss the vegetables from the skillet into the dry ingredients to coat. Stir in the melted butter and then stir in the egg.

Pour in the beer and stir until the dry ingredients are hydrated and a batter forms. Transfer the batter to the baking pan. Bake for about 25 minutes, until a toothpick inserted in the center comes out clean.

Let the loaf cool for 30 minutes before inverting the pan to remove the loaf. Slice and serve.

 **Find a Beer:** Anchor Brewing Company Summer Wheat, Bell's Brewery Oberon Ale, Odell Brewing Company Easy Street Wheat

Hearty Oatmeal Stout Quick Bread

This quick bread has a touch of sweetness from the oatmeal stout and brown sugar so that, when toasted and drizzled with honey or spread with jam, it becomes a delicious breakfast treat. On the other hand, it is savory enough to dip in soups and stews to complete a comforting meal on a cool evening.

MAKES 1 LOAF (ABOUT 8 SLICES)

1 cup old-fashioned oats, plus extra
    for topping
120 grams (1 cup) all-purpose flour
110 grams (1 cup) wholemeal flour
1 teaspoon baking powder
1 teaspoon fine sea salt
8 tablespoons (1 stick) unsalted
    butter, melted
3 tablespoons light brown sugar
2 large eggs
6 ounces (¾ cup) oatmeal stout

Preheat the oven to 375°F. Grease an 8½-by-4½-inch loaf pan with butter.

Stir together the oats, flours, baking powder, and salt in a small bowl. Add the butter and brown sugar to a large bowl and stir well. Stir in the eggs until all ingredients are combined.

Add about one-third of the dry ingredients and stir well. Next add one-third of the beer and continue to alternate with dry ingredients and beer until everything is blended into a batter.

Pour the batter into the prepared loaf pan and sprinkle the top with oats. Bake for 30 to 35 minutes until a toothpick inserted into the center comes out clean. If the bread begins to brown too rapidly during baking, cover it with a tented piece of aluminum foil about halfway through the baking time.

Let the loaf cool for 30 minutes before inverting it to remove it from the pan. Slice and serve.

Find a Beer: Anderson Valley Brewing Company Barney Flats Oatmeal Stout, Breckenridge Brewery Oatmeal Stout, Rogue Ales Shakespeare Stout

Tropical IPA Pineapple Coconut Bread

This bread allows you to turn the familiar flavors of a piña colada into a bread that can be served for breakfast or dessert. Instead of rum, a fruity IPA is blended into the batter. I like to use a mango- or pineapple-infused IPA, because the sweetness and flavor of the fruit help balance the slight bitterness that is created by the stronger hop influences of the beer.

MAKES 1 LOAF (8 TO 10 SLICES)

240 grams (2 cups) all-purpose flour

1 teaspoon baking powder

½ teaspoon baking soda

½ teaspoon fine sea salt

1 cup canned pineapple chunks, drained and chopped

1 cup granulated sugar

¼ cup melted virgin (unrefined) coconut oil

2 large eggs

⅓ cup unsweetened shredded coconut

6 ounces (¾ cup) tropical IPA

Preheat the oven to 375°F. Grease a 9-by-5-inch loaf pan with butter or coconut oil.

Stir together the flour, baking powder, baking soda, and salt in a small bowl. Toss the pineapple in the dry ingredients to coat each piece.

Add the sugar and coconut oil to a large bowl and stir to mix well. Mix in the eggs until all ingredients are combined, and then stir in the coconut.

Add about one-third of the dry ingredients and stir well. Next add one-third of the beer and continue to alternate with dry ingredients and beer until everything is blended into a batter. Pour the batter into the prepared loaf pan.

Bake for 35 to 40 minutes, until a toothpick inserted into the center comes out clean. Let the loaf cool for 30 minutes before inverting the pan to remove the loaf. Slice and serve.

 **Find a Beer:** Kona Brewing Company Hanalei IPA, Sierra Nevada Brewing Company Tropical Torpedo, SweetWater Brewing Company TripleTail

Saison Sunshine Bread

The idea for this bread was inspired by traditional Morning Glory muffins. To be honest, I was never a fan of the muffins, but I found that re-creating them in a bread form that calls for a brightly flavored saison changes them for the better. This version tastes more like a fruity carrot cake that can easily pass for a welcomed dessert.

MAKES 1 LOAF (8 TO 10 SLICES)

120 grams (1 cup) all-purpose flour

113 grams (1 cup) white whole wheat flour

1 teaspoon baking powder

1 teaspoon fine sea salt

½ teaspoon baking soda

½ teaspoon ground cinnamon

1 cup diced apple (about 1 medium apple)

⅓ cup golden raisins

1 cup light brown sugar

4 tablespoons (½ stick) unsalted butter, melted

½ cup crushed pineapple, drained

⅓ cup shredded carrots

2 large eggs

1 teaspoon vanilla extract

6 ounces (¾ cup) saison (preferably one infused with tropical fruits)

Preheat the oven to 375°F. Grease a 9-by-5-inch loaf pan with butter.

Toss together the flours, baking powder, salt, baking soda, and cinnamon in a medium bowl. Add the apple and raisins and stir to coat the fruit.

Stir together the brown sugar and butter in a large bowl. Fold in the pineapple and shredded carrots. Mix in the eggs until the mixture is smooth and then add the vanilla.

Add about one-third of the dry ingredients and stir well. Next add one-third of the beer and continue to alternate with dry ingredients and beer until everything is blended into a batter. Pour the batter into the prepared loaf pan.

Bake for 40 to 45 minutes, until a toothpick inserted into the center comes out clean. Let the loaf cool for 30 minutes before inverting the pan to remove the loaf. Slice and serve.

Find a Beer: Brewery Vivant Tropical Saison, Kona Brewing Magic Sands Mango Saison, Uinta Brewing Farmside Saison

Brown Ale Apple Bread

This recipe uses a nutty brown ale with shredded apples and walnuts to create a tender bread with the flavors of fall. Serve it warm and topped with a scoop of ice cream for dessert, or spread it with a spoonful of Porter Cinnamon Caramel Spread (page 197) and enjoy it with brunch.

MAKES 1 LOAF (8 TO 10 SLICES)

120 grams (1 cup) all-purpose flour

113 grams (1 cup) white whole wheat flour

1 teaspoon baking powder

1 teaspoon fine sea salt

½ teaspoon baking soda

½ teaspoon ground allspice

½ teaspoon ground cinnamon

1 cup shredded apple (about 1 medium apple)

⅓ cup chopped raw walnuts

1 cup light brown sugar

4 tablespoons (½ stick) unsalted butter, melted

2 large eggs

1 teaspoon vanilla extract

6 ounces (¾ cup) brown ale

TOPPING

⅓ cup all-purpose flour

¼ cup packed light brown sugar

¼ teaspoon ground cinnamon

¼ teaspoon fine sea salt

2 tablespoons cold unsalted butter, chopped

Preheat the oven to 375°F. Grease a 9-by-5-inch loaf pan with butter.

Stir together the flours, baking powder, salt, baking soda, allspice, and cinnamon in a medium bowl. Add the apple and walnuts and toss to coat with the dry ingredients.

Stir together the brown sugar and butter in a large bowl. Mix in the eggs until smooth and then add the vanilla.

Add about one-third of the dry ingredients and stir well. Next add one-third of the beer and continue to alternate with dry ingredients and beer until everything is blended into a batter. Pour the batter into the prepared loaf pan.

To make the topping, stir together the flour, brown sugar, cinnamon, and salt in a small bowl. Add the butter and use a fork to mash the butter into the other ingredients. Continue to mix until the topping is crumbly and the butter is evenly distributed in small pieces. Sprinkle the topping evenly over the batter.

Bake for 40 to 45 minutes, until a toothpick inserted into the center comes out clean. Let the loaf cool for 30 minutes before inverting the pan to remove the loaf. Slice and serve.

Find a Beer: Avery Brewing Company Ellie's Brown, Cigar City Brewing Company Maduro, Lost Coast Brewery Downtown Brown

Coconut Porter Macadamia Nut Banana Bread

I'd always thought of banana bread as rather dry and unexciting, until we traveled to Hawaii. The tender loaves they bake there—loaded with banana and often with a surprise of macadamia nuts—completely changed my view. From that point, I've worked to make banana bread much more enjoyable! This version uses a coconut porter that gives a flavor boost to the banana, coconut oil, and shredded coconut. The result is a loaf that feels like a true treat, and not simply an outlet for using bananas that are past their prime. If you can't find a coconut porter, look for a plain porter or one infused with vanilla

MAKES 1 LOAF (8 TO 10 SLICES)

120 grams (1 cup) all-purpose flour

113 grams (1 cup) white whole wheat flour

1 teaspoon baking powder

1 teaspoon fine sea salt

½ teaspoon baking soda

1½ cups mashed ripe bananas (about 3 medium bananas)

⅓ cup unsweetened shredded coconut

¼ cup melted virgin (unrefined) coconut oil

1 cup light brown sugar

2 large eggs

1 teaspoon vanilla extract

6 ounces (¾ cup) coconut porter

⅓ cup salted macadamia nuts, chopped

Preheat the oven to 375°F. Grease a 9-by-5-inch loaf pan with butter or coconut oil.

Toss together the flours, baking powder, salt, and baking soda in a medium bowl and set it aside.

Stir together the banana and coconut in a large bowl. Stir in the coconut oil and then the brown sugar until smooth. Mix in the eggs. Add the vanilla.

Add about one-third of the dry ingredients and stir well. Next add one-third of the beer and continue to alternate with dry ingredients and beer until everything is blended into a batter. Pour the batter into the prepared loaf pan. Sprinkle the top with the nuts.

Bake for 50 to 55 minutes until the loaf is golden brown and a toothpick inserted into the center comes out clean. After about 15 minutes, lay a tent of aluminum foil over the bread for the remainder of the baking time to keep the nuts from getting too dark and roasted.

Allow the loaf to cool in the pan for about 30 minutes, then carefully invert the loaf to release it from the pan. Slice and serve warm or at room temperature.

Find a Beer: Breckenridge Brewery Vanilla Porter, Maui Brewing Company Coconut Hiwa Porter, Oskar Blues Brewing Company Death by Coconut

Scotch Ale Zucchini Pecan Bread

If you are a vegetable gardener, you are likely familiar with having way too much zucchini on your hands. This recipe comes to the rescue with a boozy twist that sets it apart from traditional zucchini breads. The caramel notes of a Scotch ale go well with the hints of nutmeg and vanilla that hit the taste buds with each bite.

MAKES 1 LOAF (8 TO 10 SLICES)

120 grams (1 cup) all-purpose flour

113 grams (1 cup) white whole wheat flour

1 teaspoon baking powder

1 teaspoon fine sea salt

½ teaspoon baking soda

¼ teaspoon ground nutmeg

½ cup raw pecan halves

½ cup granulated sugar

½ cup light brown sugar

4 tablespoons (½ stick) unsalted butter, melted

2 large eggs

1 teaspoon vanilla extract

1½ cups shredded zucchini

6 ounces (¾ cup) Scotch ale

Preheat the oven to 375°F. Grease a 9-by-5-inch loaf pan with butter.

Toss together the flours, baking powder, salt, baking soda, and ground nutmeg in a medium bowl. Stir in the pecans to coat them with the dry ingredients.

Stir together the sugars and butter in a large bowl until smooth. Mix in the eggs and then the vanilla. Stir in the zucchini.

Add about one-third of the dry ingredients and stir well. Next add one-third of the beer and continue to alternate with dry ingredients and beer until everything is blended into a batter. Pour the batter into the prepared loaf pan.

Bake for 40 to 45 minutes until the loaf is golden brown and a toothpick inserted into the center comes out clean.

Allow the loaf to cool in the pan for about 30 minutes, then carefully invert the loaf to release it from the pan. Slice and serve warm or at room temperature.

Find a Beer: Great Divide Brewing Company Claymore Scotch Ale, Oskar Blues Brewing Company Old Chub, Pike Brewing Company Kilt Lifter

Spiced Pear and Witbier Loaf

This recipe is sure to become a seasonal favorite. It is loaded with aromatic spices that blend with the herbal notes of a witbier. The vibrant beer creates a light batter that blankets the tender pieces of fresh pear. Feel free to make this loaf without nuts, but walnuts do make a nice addition for both flavor and texture.

MAKES 1 LOAF (8 TO 10 SLICES)

226 grams (2 cups) white whole wheat flour

2 teaspoons baking powder

1 teaspoon ground cinnamon

1 teaspoon fine sea salt

½ teaspoon ground allspice

½ teaspoon ground cardamom

½ teaspoon ground ginger

¼ teaspoon ground cloves

¼ teaspoon ground coriander

1 firm pear, cored and chopped

⅓ cup chopped raw walnuts

1 cup sugar

8 tablespoons (1 stick) unsalted butter, melted

2 large eggs

1 teaspoon vanilla extract

6 ounces (¾ cup) witbier

Preheat the oven to 375°F. Grease a 9-by-5-inch loaf pan with butter.

Stir together the flour, baking powder, cinnamon, salt, allspice, cardamom, ginger, cloves, and coriander in a medium bowl. Toss in the pear and walnuts to coat with the dry ingredients.

Add the sugar and butter to a large bowl and stir until smooth. Mix in the eggs and then the vanilla.

Stir in about one-third of the dry ingredients. Next add one-third of the beer and continue to alternate with dry ingredients and beer until everything is blended into a batter. Pour the batter into the prepared loaf pan.

Bake for 40 to 45 minutes until the loaf is golden brown and a toothpick inserted into the center comes out clean. If the bread begins to brown too rapidly during baking, cover it with a tented piece of aluminum foil about halfway through the baking time.

Allow the loaf to cool in the pan for about 30 minutes, then carefully invert the loaf to release it from the pan. Slice and serve warm or at room temperature.

Find a Beer: Avery Brewing Company White Rascal, Bell's Brewery Winter White Ale, Cigar City Brewing Company Florida Cracker

Strawberry Blonde Pistachio Bread

As the strawberries warm in the oven, the inviting aroma of this bread fills the whole kitchen. It's warm, comforting, and summery all at the same time! You can pair strawberries with any kind of nut, but I think pistachios go especially well in this bread. The recipe uses a blonde ale, and if you happen to come across a strawberry blonde ale, be sure to use that. Other strawberry beers, like wheat ales, are good choices too. Strawberries happen to be the favorite people-food of our pug, Macy, and while this bread is for humans only, she always gets a few strawberries when I make it. This recipe is dedicated to her.

MAKES 1 LOAF (8 TO 10 SLICES)

120 grams (1 cup) all-purpose flour

113 grams (1 cup) white whole wheat flour

1 teaspoon baking powder

1 teaspoon fine sea salt

½ teaspoon baking soda

¾ cup diced firm strawberries (about 5 large strawberries)

⅓ cup roasted, shelled pistachios

1 cup sugar

4 tablespoons (½ stick) unsalted butter, melted

2 large eggs

1 teaspoon vanilla extract

¾ cup mashed ripe strawberries (about 5 large strawberries; see Note)

6 ounces (¾ cup) blonde ale

Preheat the oven to 375°F. Grease a 9-by-5-inch loaf pan with butter.

Toss together the flours, baking powder, salt, and baking soda in a medium bowl. Gently stir in the diced strawberries and pistachios to coat both with the dry ingredients.

Stir together the sugar and melted butter in a large bowl. Stir in the eggs and vanilla until smooth. Fold in the mashed strawberries.

Add about one-third of the dry ingredients and stir well. Next add one-third of the beer and continue to alternate with dry ingredients and beer until everything is blended into a batter. Pour the batter into the prepared loaf pan.

Bake for 40 to 45 minutes until the loaf is golden brown and a toothpick inserted into the center comes out clean.

Allow the loaf to cool in the pan for about 30 minutes, then carefully invert the loaf to release it from the pan. Slice and serve warm or at room temperature.

Find a Beer: Arbor Brewing Company Strawberry Blonde, Lancaster Brewing Company Strawberry Wheat, Big Sky Brewing Company Summer Honey

Note: If you can't find softer, ripe berries, chop firm berries and then sprinkle them with a teaspoon or two from the 1 cup of sugar, and let them sit for about 30 minutes. They'll soften and become easy to mash.

Pumpkin Ale Ginger Loaf

Autumn is not complete without at least one slice of pumpkin bread. This recipe takes a classic and enhances the seasonal flavors with pumpkin ale and candied ginger. If you can't find a pumpkin ale, any type of spiced autumn beer or holiday spiced ale works well. If you have a craving for it outside of autumn, use a brown or amber ale.

MAKES 1 LOAF (8 TO 10 SLICES)

240 grams (2 cups) all-purpose flour
2 teaspoons baking powder
1 teaspoon fine sea salt
½ teaspoon ground cinnamon
½ teaspoon grated fresh ginger root
½ teaspoon ground nutmeg
¼ teaspoon ground cloves
¼ cup finely chopped candied ginger
1¼ cups sugar
8 tablespoons (1 stick) unsalted butter, melted
2 large eggs
1 cup pumpkin puree
6 ounces (¾ cup) pumpkin ale

Preheat the oven to 375°F. Grease a 9-by-5-inch loaf pan with butter.

Stir together the flour, baking powder, salt, cinnamon, ginger root, nutmeg, and cloves in a medium bowl. Toss in the candied ginger to coat it with the dry ingredients.

Add the sugar and butter to a large bowl and stir until smooth. Mix in the eggs and then stir in the pumpkin puree.

Mix in about one-third of the dry ingredients. Next add one-third of the beer and continue to alternate with dry ingredients and beer until everything is blended into a batter. Pour the batter into the prepared loaf pan.

Bake for 40 to 45 minutes until the loaf is golden brown and a toothpick inserted into the center comes out clean. If the bread begins to brown too rapidly during baking, cover it with a tented piece of aluminum foil for the last 10 minutes of baking.

Allow the loaf to cool in the pan for about 30 minutes, then carefully invert the loaf to release it from the pan. Slice and serve warm or at room temperature.

Find a Beer: Epic Brewing The Gourdian, Rogue Ales Pumpkin Patch Ale, Uinta Brewing Company Pumpkin Ale

Salted Lime Gose Bread

I consider the gose to be a completely unique style in craft beer. It has the tartness of a sour, but with a saltiness that balances the pucker. When I'm not drinking one, I like to use the style in making citrus breads. This one plays on those salty notes by working sea salt into the batter and the topping. Goses can be found infused with a variety of fruit flavors. Look for a plain gose or a lime version for this recipe.

MAKES 1 LOAF (8 SLICES)

210 grams (1¾ cups) all-purpose
    flour
1 teaspoon baking powder
1 tablespoon lime zest
½ teaspoon fine sea salt
1¼ cups sugar
½ pound (2 sticks) unsalted butter,
    softened
2 large eggs
1 tablespoon fresh lime juice
6 ounces (¾ cup) gose

GLAZE
¼ cup powdered sugar, sifted
2 teaspoons fresh lime juice
¼ teaspoon lime zest
⅛ teaspoon fine sea salt

Preheat the oven to 350°F. Grease an 8½-by-4½-inch loaf pan with butter.

Toss together the flour, baking powder, lime zest, and salt in a small bowl. Stir together the sugar and butter in a large bowl. Mix in the eggs and then the lime juice.

Stir about one-third of the dry ingredients into the wet ingredients. Next add one-third of the beer and continue to alternate with dry ingredients and beer until everything is blended into a batter. Pour the batter into the prepared loaf pan.

Bake for 30 to 35 minutes until a toothpick inserted into the center comes out clean.

Allow the loaf to cool in the pan for about 30 minutes, then carefully invert the loaf to release it from the pan. Let it cool completely on a cooling rack.

For the glaze, stir together the powdered sugar and lime juice in a small dish until smooth. Toss together the zest and salt in a small dish. Set the cooling rack over a piece of wax paper or parchment paper to catch glaze that drips down.

Drizzle the loaf with the glaze and then sprinkle with the zest and salt. Let the glaze set up for 5 minutes before slicing to serve.

Find a Beer: Anderson Valley Brewing Company The Kimmie, The Yink & The Holy Gose, Victory Brewing Company Limey Gose, Sierra Nevada Brewing Company Otra Vez Lime & Agave

Chocolate Stout Peanut Butter Bread

This recipe is a sweet twist on classic beer bread. It is so simple to make and can be served for breakfast or dessert. Classic beer breads tend to hold up best among other quick breads for flavor, so it is also a great option if you need a sweet treat to give as a gift or to take along to a party.

MAKES 1 LOAF (8 TO 10 SLICES)

339 grams (3 cups) self-rising flour
½ cup creamy peanut butter
⅓ cup granulated sugar
12 ounces (1½ cups) chocolate stout
½ cup semi-sweet chocolate chunks

Preheat the oven to 375°F. Grease a 9-by-5-inch loaf pan with butter.

Stir together the flour and peanut butter in a large bowl, using a fork to mash it together, until the peanut butter is distributed throughout in small pieces. Stir in the sugar.

Pour in the beer and stir until all ingredients are combined into a batter. Fold in the chocolate chunks.

Transfer the batter to the prepared loaf pan. Bake for 35 minutes, until a toothpick inserted into the center comes out clean. Let the loaf cool in the pan for at least 30 minutes. Invert the pan to remove the loaf. Let it cool to room temperature before slicing to serve.

Find a Beer: Belching Beaver Brewery Peanut Butter Milk Stout, Rogue Ales Chocolate Stout, Samuel Adams Brewmasters Collection Cream Stout

Salted Dark Chocolate Cherry Fruit Ale Bread

This sweet dessert bread is as rich and chocolatey as it looks! It uses frozen cherries so you can make it any time of year. You also have a lot of flexibility with beer choice to enhance the delicious flavors. A cherry-infused fruit ale such as a cherry wheat is a good choice, but don't be afraid to go bold and dark. A stout, such as a berry- and chocolate-infused stout, is another ideal option.

MAKES 1 LOAF (8 TO 10 SLICES)

300 grams (2½ cups) all-purpose flour
1 teaspoon baking powder
1 teaspoon fine sea salt
⅓ cup cocoa powder
¼ cup cherry juice (from the thawed cherries)
1 cup sugar
8 tablespoons (1 stick) unsalted butter, melted
2 large eggs
6 ounces (¾ cup) fruit ale or fruit stout
1 cup frozen dark, sweet cherries, thawed and chopped
1 cup semi-sweet chocolate chunks
Flaked sea salt

Preheat the oven to 375°F. Grease an 8½-by-4½-inch loaf pan with butter.

Toss together the flour, baking powder, and sea salt in a medium bowl. Stir together the cocoa powder and cherry juice in a small dish until a thick chocolate paste forms.

Stir together the sugar and butter in a large bowl. Mix in the chocolate paste until smooth and then mix in the eggs.

Add about one-third of the beer and stir well, then add in one-third of the dry ingredients. Continue to alternate with beer and dry ingredients until everything is blended into a batter. Pour half of the batter in the pan. Sprinkle with all of the chopped cherries and half of the chocolate chunks.

Pour in the rest of the batter. Top with the remaining chocolate chunks and a sprinkle of flaked sea salt.

Bake for 40 to 45 minutes, until a toothpick inserted into the center comes out clean. Sprinkle with a little more flaked salt as soon as you remove it from the oven. Allow the loaf to cool for 30 minutes until it is easily removed from the pan by inverting it, then slice to serve.

Find a Beer: Bell's Brewery Cherry Stout, O'Fallon Cherry Chocolate Beer, Samuel Adams Cherry Wheat

Chapter 8

SPREAD IT ON
CRAFT BEER BREAD SPREADS AND TOPPERS

I think all of the breads in this book are fully enjoyable on their own, but a spread here, a dollop of jam there, or a dip served alongside certainly doesn't hurt. These are some of my favorite spreads and toppers made better with beer. These recipes make small batches meant to be served with a loaf of your choice and are not prepared for long-term storage. Be sure to use them up within three to five days of making them.

Classic Kentucky Beer Cheese

About eight years ago, when we lived in Kentucky, I was asked to judge a beer cheese competition. I had no idea there were so many versions, and I'll admit that after about 20, they all started to run together. But the experience did help me identify what I like in a beer cheese, and this version sums it up. It has a bit of texture, which is achieved by using a freshly shredded medium or sharp Cheddar. Slightly tangy and a bit spicy are also requirements. You also must be able to taste the beer! So, while American light lagers are often used in classic recipes, I prefer a bold pale ale or an IPA. Serve this beer cheese with the Sesame Flatbread Beer Crackers (page 146) or with carrot sticks and celery.

MAKES ABOUT 3½ CUPS

20 ounces sharp or medium
   Cheddar, shredded
2 garlic cloves, minced
2 teaspoons Worcestershire sauce
2 teaspoons hot sauce
½ teaspoon dry mustard powder
¼ teaspoon fine sea salt
¼ teaspoon ground black pepper
12 ounces (1½ cups) IPA or pale ale
Smoked paprika for garnish

Add the cheese, garlic, Worcestershire sauce, hot sauce, mustard powder, salt, and pepper to a food processor. Secure the lid and pulse in 5-second intervals until the ingredients are combined, five to six times.

With the processor on, pour the beer through the liquid spout on the machine and blend until the ingredients combine into a beer cheese that is spreadable, about 30 seconds.

It can be served right away, but it is better if it sits in the refrigerator to firm up for 1 hour or 2 to allow the flavors to blend. Garnish with smoked paprika before serving.

Find a Beer: Deschutes Brewery Fresh Squeezed IPA, West Sixth Brewing Pennyrile Pale Ale, Yazoo Brewing Pale Ale

Vienna Lager Veggie Smoked Cheddar Spread

Veggie cream cheese is my top pick as a spread for bread. I think it is made even better when a smoky Cheddar is blended in, and that is what I do with this recipe. I like to use a crisp, slightly sweet Vienna lager to add creaminess and to bring the flavors together. If you can't find this style, a märzen or okto-berfest would work well, nor would I shy away from a bolder pale ale for something different. Give this spread at least 1 hour in the fridge before serving so the flavors can blend and it can firm up to become more spreadable. I like to pair this with the Pale Ale Sandwich Loaf (page 88).

MAKES ABOUT 2¼ CUPS

8 ounces cream cheese, softened
6 ounces smoked Cheddar, shredded
6 ounces (¾ cup) Vienna lager
½ cup shredded carrots
½ cup finely chopped spinach
4 scallions, sliced
1 tablespoon roughly chopped fresh dill
¼ teaspoon fine sea salt

Cut the cream cheese into pieces and add them to a food processor. Add the shredded Cheddar. Pulse a few times to combine so that the cheeses are mixed, but crumbly. Pour in the beer and process on low for 45 seconds, until blended.

Add the carrots, spinach, scallions, dill, and salt. Use five to seven short pulses to combine all the ingredients and to chop the veggies. It should become thin but spreadable, with pieces of vegetables evenly distributed throughout.

Transfer the spread to a container with a lid. Cover and refrigerate for 1 hour before serving.

Find a Beer: Samuel Adams Boston Lager, Sierra Nevada Brewing Company Vienna, Uinta Brewing Yard Sale

Märzen Caramelized Onion Butter

There are few things as deeply flavored as caramelized onions that have been cooked in a malty beer that hints at toasty caramel notes. This recipe takes those onions and blends them with butter to create a spread that melts like velvet onto a slice of toasted bread or a warm roll. It makes a great addition to the Whole Grain Irish Stout Rolls (page 74).

MAKES ABOUT 1¼ CUPS

½ pound (2 sticks) unsalted butter, softened at room temperature
1 small yellow onion, sliced
6 ounces (¾ cup) märzen
¼ teaspoon flaked smoked sea salt

Add 1 tablespoon of the butter to a medium skillet. Melt over medium heat. Add the onion and reduce the heat to medium-low. Cook for 10 minutes, stirring occasionally. The onions will just be beginning to brown. Carefully add the beer. Increase the heat to medium so that the beer begins to simmer. Cook to evaporate the liquid, about 8 more minutes, stirring often. The onions will become brown and jam-like.

Reduce the heat to low and continue to cook for 3 to 5 more minutes, stirring constantly, to further soften the onions. They should break apart easily with a rubber spatula. Set them aside to cool for 10 minutes.

Transfer the onions to a cutting board and chop finely. Place the remaining softened butter in a medium bowl. Add the onions to the bowl along with the smoked sea salt. Stir well to combine. The butter should be stored in the refrigerator, but allow it to soften at room temperature before serving.

Find a Beer: Flying Dog Brewery Dogtoberfest Märzen, Great Lakes Brewing Company Oktoberfest, Sierra Nevada Brewing Company Oktoberfest

Gose Chutney

Gose adds a tartness to this chutney that balances the sweetness of the apple and the savory notes of the yellow onion. When cooled, the syrup coats the fruits to create a relish-like topping that is ideal for the English Bitter English Muffins (page 49) or when served alongside the Curry Chickpea–Topped Lager Flatbread with Yogurt Tahini Sauce (page 137).

MAKES ABOUT 1 CUP

2 cups peeled, diced apples (about 2 medium apples)
⅓ cup yellow onion, chopped
⅓ cup golden raisins
1 tablespoon minced fresh ginger root
1 cup brown sugar
¼ teaspoon crushed red pepper
¼ teaspoon fine sea salt
6 ounces (¾ cup) gose

Stir together all ingredients in a large saucepan. Bring to a boil over medium heat. Watch it closely and adjust the heat as needed to prevent it from boiling over the sides. Stir occasionally and cook until the apples are soft and the sauces are thickened, about 30 minutes. Stir often during the last 10 minutes of cooking to make sure it doesn't burn along the bottom. Let it sit for 10 minutes on the stove.

Transfer the chutney to a bowl with a lid. Cover and refrigerate it until it's completely chilled, about 1 hour, before serving.

Find a Beer: Anderson Valley Brewing Company, The Kimmie, The Yink & The Holy Gose, Avery Brewing Company El Gose, Westbrook Brewing Company Gose

Belgian Blonde Ale Beer Jelly

The idea of making jelly out of beer is one that is simply too intriguing not to try. A Belgian blonde ale is low in bitterness, and when cooked with sugar it creates a jelly that brightens any bread or baked good. I like to spread it on the Classic Beer Bread Vanilla Scones with Honey Glaze (page 28). If you can't find that style, I also enjoy making this with a hefeweizen.

MAKES ABOUT 1 CUP

12 ounces (1½ cups) Belgian blonde ale
1½ cups sugar
1 tablespoon apple cider vinegar
One 3-ounce pouch liquid fruit pectin

Add the beer to a 5- or 6-quart soup pot. Let it rest for 5 minutes to allow the foam to settle. Stir in the sugar and vinegar, and then the pectin.

Turn the heat to medium and continue to stir to dissolve the sugar. Bring it to a boil, watching it closely. The beer will foam up and you may need to lower the heat to prevent it from boiling over. Stir occasionally and let it boil for 10 to 15 minutes.

As it nears 10 minutes, begin to stir more often. It is ready when it begins to thicken and the streaks made on the bottom and sides of the pot as you stir hold longer before the jelly fills them back in. It will coat a spoon in a thin sauce.

Pour the jelly into a clean, heat-proof pint jar. It will have reduced down to just about 8 ounces, maybe a little more depending on your cooking time. Let it cool for 10 more minutes. Remove and discard any foam that has settled on top. Secure the lid and refrigerate the jelly until it's well chilled, 4 to 6 hours. It will thicken as it cools into a slightly firm but spreadable jelly. Stir gently to break it up when setting it out to serve.

Find a Beer: The Lost Abbey Devotion Blonde Ale, Uinta Brewing Monkshine Belgian Style Blonde Ale, Sierra Nevada Brewing Company Kellerweis

Strawberry Coriander Witbier Jam

This sweet summer jam combines seasonal fruit with coriander. The citrus and herbal spice notes of a witbier work with these ingredients to create a jam that feels familiar, but with a hint of flavor that sparks curiosity. Use this jam to give the Strawberry Blonde Pistachio Bread (page 170) an extra boost of fruit flavor.

MAKES ABOUT 2 CUPS

1 pound strawberries, hulled and halved
6 ounces (¾ cup) witbier
1 cup sugar
½ teaspoon ground coriander
Pinch of fine sea salt

Add the strawberries, beer, and sugar to a food processor. Pulse in 5-second bursts until the strawberries are finely chopped, about five times. Transfer to a 5- or 6-quart soup pot.

Bring the mixture to a boil over medium heat. Watch it closely; as it reaches about 5 minutes it will foam up and you will need to reduce the heat to prevent it from boiling over. Continue to adjust the heat as needed to maintain a boil. Stir occasionally.

Boil for about 15 more minutes, until the jam becomes thick. Stir it often at this point. During this process, place a small plate in the freezer for 5 minutes. Spoon a small amount of jam on the plate and return it to the freezer for 2 minutes. If it has set up on the plate and is not runny, the jam is done. If it's still runny, continue to boil until it sets up on the plate when tested.

Remove the jam from the heat. Stir in the coriander and salt. Pour the jam into a heat-safe pint jar with a lid. Let it cool for 5 minutes. Secure the lid and place it in the refrigerator to cool completely, about 2 hours.

Find a Beer: Avery Brewing Company White Rascal, Breckenridge Brewery White Ale, Door County Brewing Company Little Sister Witbier

Chocolate Almond Stout Spread

The slight coffee bitterness of a stout blends with sweet chocolate in this spread. I like to pulse the almonds until they create a grainy powder so that the spread has a bit of texture from the fine pieces of nuts. Let this spread cool in the fridge for at least 6 hours so that it will thicken before serving. It makes a great topper for the Hearty Oatmeal Stout Quick Bread (page 157).

MAKES ABOUT 1⅓ CUPS

6 ounces (¾ cup) stout

½ cup sugar

1 tablespoon unsweetened cocoa powder

5 ounces semi-sweet chocolate, chopped

3 tablespoons unsalted butter, cubed and softened

¼ teaspoon almond extract

½ cup whole raw almonds, chopped until nearly a fine powder (see Note)

Stir together the stout, sugar, and cocoa powder in a medium saucepan over medium heat until all ingredients are smooth. Bring it to a simmer and then remove the pan from the heat.

Stir in the chocolate and butter until they're melted and then stir in the almond extract and almonds. Pour the spread into a jar with a lid. Secure the lid and refrigerate the spread until it's chilled and spreadable, about 3 hours. Stir well before serving.

Find a Beer: Bell's Brewery Kalamazoo Stout, Deschutes Brewery Obsidian Stout, Sierra Nevada Brewing Company Stout

Note: I pulse the almonds in a single-serve blender. I stop when they turn into a powder, just short of them turning into a pureed almond butter.

Porter Cinnamon Caramel Spread

The hint of cinnamon in this spread makes it a nice addition to holiday celebrations. It is rich with the roasted flavors of a porter and the deep sweetness of brown sugar. When warm, the caramel is more like a sauce, but once chilled for about 6 hours it spreads easily to create a delicious topping for both yeast breads and quick breads. Serve it with the Cinnamon Raisin Walnut Brown Ale Bread (page 96) or the Brown Ale Apple Bread (page 162).

MAKES ABOUT 1 CUP

½ cup heavy cream
½ cup light brown sugar
¼ cup granulated sugar
6 ounces (¾ cup) porter
4 tablespoons (½ stick) unsalted butter, cubed and softened
¼ teaspoon vanilla extract
¼ teaspoon ground cinnamon
¼ teaspoon fine sea salt

Stir together the cream, brown sugar, and granulated sugar in a medium saucepan over medium heat until smooth, about 1 minute. Remove the pan from the heat and stir in the beer.

Return the pan to medium heat and bring the liquid to a boil. Boil for 15 minutes, until a candy thermometer reaches about 218°F and the caramel has thickened. Remove it from the heat and stir in the butter until it's melted. Add the vanilla, cinnamon, and salt, and stir well.

Transfer the spread to a heat-safe jar with a lid. Let it cool for 15 minutes. Secure the lid and transfer it to the refrigerator to cool until it's thick and spreadable, about 6 hours.

Find a Beer: Anchor Brewing Company Anchor Porter, Founders Brewing Company Robust Porter, Sierra Nevada Brewing Company Porter

ACKNOWLEDGMENTS

Thank you to everyone who supported my last book, *Food on Tap*, and for your excitement around the release of *Beer Bread*. You made writing my second book even more fun. Thank you to my recipe testers and to those who assisted with the photos. Your help was essential and greatly appreciated. Thanks to my agent Leslie Stoker for believing that I had another book to write and for the team at The Countryman Press who worked to bring this book to life. Thank you to my husband, Dan, for putting up with tables upon tables of bread filling the kitchen every night and for never becoming discouraged despite regular announcements that we were having beer bread for dinner. It's because of you that I get to do the work that I enjoy so much.

INDEX